# Anti Hacking Security: Fight Data Breach

**The Incredible** Detect Remove
    **Approach to fight data breach**

## Mr. Vivek Ashvinbhai Pancholi

B.E.(Computer), ICSI | CNSS, NSE 3, ISO 27001 Lead Auditor

Copyright © 2023 Vivek Ashvinbhai Pancholi.

All rights reserved. This book or any portion thereof may not be reproduced, modified, transferred or used in any manner without the express written permission of the Publisher and Author except for the authorized ones or the use of brief quotation in a book review.

For the permission to use portion of the book in commercial purpose, contact **Mr. Vivek Ashvinbhai Pancholi** and/or **The VP Techno Labs® International**

1st edition 2023

www.myvptechnolabs.com

# Legal Disclaimer

To protect the privacy of certain individuals, organizations and companies, the names and identifying details have been changed to generic and redacted. However the stories and scenarios are based on real incidents, facts. If readers (Whether they are individuals, Businesses, Governments or any other category) wish to apply the strategies mentioned in the book, they can! But at their own risk. The Authors, Publishers, Editors and Owners are not responsible for any type of damage. Authors and Team take proper care while writing this book, however it doesn't guarantee a 100% perfect or error-free. The Author and Team welcomes recommendations from the readers' side. We respect state, central and international laws and rights. Here Mr. Yash's name is taken as an example and illustration purpose. The name Mr. Yash used here is fictitious. Only peoples, organizations names and identity are fictitious. It is because of privacy and identity protection purposes.

## About the Author

## Mr. VIVEK ASHVINBHAI PANCHOLI

Vivek Ashvinbhai Pancholi is multi award winning cybersecurity consultant. He completed his B.E(Computer) from Gujarat Technological University in Y-2019. He won several international awards and recognition for his incredible contribution towards cybersecurity.

He Helped to secure 50+ Fortune Top 500 companies, International Governments, International law enforcement agencies and secured 300+ Top international companies. His expertise includes Anti Hacking security, Penetration Testing, Red Teaming, Digital Forensics & Crime Detection, Business Disaster Recovery Planning, and Breach Incident Management. He wrote this book intended to solve the most challenging problem and helps every organization who is facing, "Data Breach".

# Acknowledgement

This book is dedicated to my old parents who love me unconditionally. I always feel proud that I have such loving and caring parents and no matter what the situation is, they stand with me and support me. And whatever I'm now and whatever I'll do, it is not possible without their blessings.

During COVID Times, I and my parents got severe illnesses along with COVID-19, Black Fungus, and some other serious lung inflammatory disease, which is not easy to cure. During this time, I realized the value of family. Even though they are 65+ years old and have some chronic health problems, they never forgot to take care of me.

I came up with the idea to write a book during the increased cyber-attacks that rise after COVID. I have seen many organizations don't take cybersecurity seriously. And that is why hackers find a way to grab that valuable stuff that is part of the business.

The statement does not only apply to businesses but of course to individuals. You'll probably think, why? Right?

Whenever people and business owners take data security as a joke. The Hacker then exploits the weakness of people and through people, they find loopholes in business, then the whole organization and its consumers.

# Introduction:

The main motive of this book is to elaborate on genuine and unshakable ways they can prevent and protect against data leaks and data breaches from beginning to advance. After reading this book, I will guarantee you or your organization implement these rules and then feel relaxed!

You cannot avoid data breaches. No system on this internet is 100% Secure. But the attempt is to **DETECT** vulnerabilities or loopholes, in other words, **REMOVE** these Detected Vulnerabilities by securing every perspective and then **ENFORCE** by applying preventive measures.

This **DETECT**, **REMOVE**, **ENFORCE** Approach not only helps businesses but also helps people to remain secure in this digital world.

The reading criteria of the book are from beginner to advanced. So anyone with basic knowledge or advanced knowledge can read this book. Not only this book covers real-life challenges and solutions that arise in cybersecurity but also is packed with long-term and great solutions that will protect and provide resistance to people and businesses against cyber threats.

This book will save millions of dollars for an organization. Not only saving money but reputation and consumers. Apart from protecting an organization, it also helps people who are smart enough but still trapped by digital intruders.

# INDEX:

- [Legal Disclaimer](#) — 3
- [About the Author](#) — 4
- [Acknowledgement](#) — 5
- [Introduction](#) — 6
- [Chapter 1: Anti Hacking Security](#) — 8
- [Chapter 2: Data Breach](#) — 13
- [Chapter 3: The DETECT REMOVE ENFORCE Approach](#) — 21
- [Chapter 4: Cybersecurity Threats](#) — 27
- [Chapter 5: Cybersecurity for Individuals](#) — 42
- [Chapter 6: Cybersecurity for Businesses](#) — 62
- [Chapter 7: How to save millions of dollars](#) — 86
- [Chapter 8: Automation & AI in cybersecurity](#) — 92
- [Chapter 9: Should you trust yourself or your consultants](#) — 105
- [Chapter 10: A Perfect Solution](#) — 109
- [References](#) — 110

# Chapter 1: Anti Hacking Security

Anti Hacking security consists of various tools and technologies that help to prevent cyber attacks in a known way. In Another way, it is a method for securing computer systems by applying multiple commonly known techniques used by hackers and cyber threats.

Usually, already different organizations and governments implemented several general remediation techniques to secure their system, But you still think cyberattacks happen, alright?

Just because they implemented several general security policies and practices, At the end of the day, cyberattacks become more sophisticated hour by hour. So they can easily defeat protection mechanisms and bypass restrictions that are generated during traditional anti-hacking implementations.

Governments and organizations think about who can hack their infrastructure if all aspects are covered by security policies and monitored by so-called cybersecurity experts! And even if hackers somehow gain an advantage and access to their data is not very important, they are likely to skip these areas. But unfortunately, hackers are always looking to take advantage of systems via weak locations. Once they enter into weak locations, they also find an absolute path to access root controls!

And after they got root-level access, they attempt to steal something important, and whoa! Data Breach happens!

Traditional Anti-Hacking Security Consists following areas:

1. Backup & Restore

2. Strong Password Policy
3. Anti-Hacking Security Software (Anti-Virus, SIEM, Vulnerability Assessment Systems, Password Managers)
4. Enhanced security access controls (MFA, Biometric, IRIS)
5. Network Security

Securing the above five critical areas doesn't ensure full-proof security. We can protect and prevent hackers from getting access to weak locations. Here's how!

## Applying Newer Anti-Hacking Security to Prevent Data Breaches.

Applying just traditional security controls is always flawed security practices. But apart from applying standard security controls with other parameters is always good.

1. Applying traditional security controls (Consider the above five)
2. Restricting internet users from accessing intranet content. Separate internet and intranet with Gateway Firewall, SIEM, and SOAR systems.
3. If you have different departments like sales and marketing. You can always separate one from another. **I.E.:** Marketing department users cannot access sales department systems. So Defining such types of access controls will help you to reduce intranet-level attacks. The same will be applied to the government also.
4. Make a standard group policy and implement it according to the department wise. Make two superusers for each department. Only those devices can access the outside department. Restrict the rest of all. Include hardware and software-based access controls. If someone from the outer department tries to insert a USB drive then access control should block access and create an incident and forward it to SIEM.
5. Perform Regular Vulnerability Assessment & Penetration Testing by the internal security team by using automatic tools and hire a dedicated cybersecurity firm to do periodic security audits carried out by their expert team.

6. Train your employees in cybersecurity awareness(For Govt. and For Private Org.)

## Why is Anti-Hacking Security important?

Anti-hacking security helps you both in post-hacking and pre-hacking scenarios. Let's understand by taking an example,

**ABC Pvt. Ltd** is an Accounting & Law firm that helps its clients to comply with governance and regulatory requirements. The size of the firm is 60 employees and has 3 departments in total. First is customer service, the second is support and the third one is for newer customers. Each department has 20 workers. And total work is online and computerized, so there is the chance to leak the data and put their clients' confidentiality at risk. So they hired a security consulting firm that implemented several in-house security appliances and applied policy to make the organization secure! Here company ABC Pvt. Ltd has used Anti-Hacking security in two ways.

1. They hired a security consulting firm, and they regularly assess their infrastructure.
2. They implemented several software and hardware-based security mechanisms.

Here ABC Pvt. Ltd company used Anti-Hacking security in pre-hacking scenarios. This means the company is not hacked or compromised but they understand the importance of digital security while serving their clients. So they take it seriously. *And they use a pre-hacking scenario.*

Let's try to understand the post-hacking scenario by taking an example,
XYZ Pvt. Ltd is a Group of Private Hospitals. It has 10 hospitals across the city and is well-equipped and has proper facilities. But they don't take cybersecurity seriously.

They organized a free camp for all the beneficiaries. For that, they opened an online portal connected to their internal database of patients. On the day of camp, they got almost 5000+ registrations for their free camp. During this period their website was hacked by ransomware and all medical records were encrypted and leaked.

So they're victims of HIPAA Violation as they don't take their patients and medical data seriously. So this incident happened. In this case, they hired a well-performing cybersecurity consulting firm to recover from the damage.

For this, the cybersecurity firm isolated their hacked systems with the internal systems and started performing cleaning and decryption operations. After the isolation procedure, they release the recovered data to the live website environment and the portal is live again. The chief security officer Mr. ABCD says there is a critical SQL Injection vulnerability in their Code, that's why hackers exploited this vulnerability and gained access to the patient's data. XYZ Pvt. Ltd has realized its mistake and agreed to implement Anti-Hacking security in its organization to prevent these types of attacks in the future.

So they implemented the following:
1. Proper Access Controls and security policies
2. Websites, Databases, and Portals monitoring software (SIEM Software)
3. Implemented HIPAA Compliance to comply with government regulatory requirements and secure patient data in a structured way.

So in this scenario, *XYZ Pvt. Ltd has used Anti-Hacking security in the post-hacking scenario.*

Anti-hacking security combination of various tools, techniques, and policies to make the digital environment unhackable. Still, we don't think it provides 100% security. Our try is to make it difficult to break security controls and proper alerting mechanisms.

So hope you understand the importance and applications of Anti-Hacking security. Anti-Hacking Security can be helpful in both a commercial way and a personal way. You also need to ensure at the personal level that your payment data and other PII data are secured.

# Chapter 2: Data Breach

A data breach is an incident when an intruder finds a path to gain unauthorized access to a particular system. The path may be vulnerable or have a weak configuration. A data breach happens at any time but mostly happens when the proper watch has not been carried out by the chief security officer(CISO is the officer who is responsible for securing the system and monitoring.). Data Breaches can be in any form like *virus infection*, *traces of intrusion attempts*, *DDoS*, *Stolen Information*, etc. Most of the breaches happened due to stolen data because stolen data helps hackers to gain access to victims' accounts.

Let's understand how data breach happens by taking an example,

## How Data Breach Happens?

Data breach happens in any form like,

1. **Virus Infection**

   Virus infection happens when the end user downloads a software program from an untrusted website or clicks on unwanted links. Whenever a user clicks on an unknown link, the opened link might redirect to the page when the user is prompted to enter personal information. If a person fills in and submits the details then the hacker gets all the information and may hack the account using personal information provided. This ultimately leads to data compromise and leads to data breaches finally. If the victim is associated with a particular organization, then hackers can also find common interests among other corporate users and also attempt to cheat them with different offers and scams. So this will be very dangerous for an organization.

## 2. Traces of Intrusion attempts

Due to different motives, hackers can choose an organization to hack their data and put their customers' privacy and data at risk. For example, XYZ group is a state-sponsored hacker group that has a political motive. So they target organizations that are in opposition's support. So there is an organization named **Alpha Pvt. Ltd that strictly** disagrees with political views. XYZ hackers group already knew it and tried to exploit the organization by sending phishing emails to the company employees. But None of the employees clicked suspicious links sent by the hackers' group. So they tried another method called **"DDoS"**.

They hacked a random number of IoT devices on the internet and made them part of a botnet network, after this the group of hackers installed RAT(Remote Access Trojans) and malware on infected IoT Devices. Now with the help of these Botnet devices hackers launched a massive **1-Tbps** Network Amplification attack on that organization's network. So all the websites were affected by this activity and went down.

Due to this activity, hackers leave traces of hacking in log files. So this ultimately leads to Denial of Service and then finally leads to a data breach.

## 3. Stolen Information

This is the most possible reason behind any data breach. Mostly the hacker groups are active on darknet forums and on these forums, the members' posts are pirated, stolen, and unauthorized content. So the previous data breach data will also be there. The Hackers program automatic software that automates some tasks like carding, brute forcing login portals, phishing campaigns, etc. Then they start targeting the victims by sending random emails and publishing their financial data online. Carding is a known technique to add and validate credit card/debit card data against various shopping sites. Stolen passwords can be used against different websites to log in on behalf of victims and access protected or authorized resources and context, which is only meant for authorized ones. So this is also the utmost reason behind the data breach.

So hope you will understand how the data breach happens. There is a genuine reason present behind the successful data breach.

You will find lots of data breaches data by searching on the internet.

## Why do hackers steal data or cause data breach?

Well, hackers have different motives behind intrusion attempts or hacking! Some of them are motivated by state-sponsored activity (Supported by state or federal government for specific reasons), Political Reason, Monetary gain reason, Personal or Corporate competition revenge, etc. Let's understand in deeply by taking proper example,

1. **State Sponsored Activity**

   The funds and resources provided by the Government to hack. Then the government provides this order in case it monitors users anonymously or conducts surveys of data usage and user activity. In this case, hackers send phishing links (Links containing malware or suspicious) to the victims. Whenever a user clicks on that link, the email redirects users to different links opened in other browsers. And the website prompts users to allow some permissions.

   If the user allows that permission, the whole device and its data are accessible. Now hackers can read users' data like phone calls, sms, videos, photos, voice mails, emails, location history, and even stored financial data(Credit/Debit Cards, Wallets). In some cases, the government also taps the phone of the end user if they suspect some illicit activity from the user's side.

2. **Political Reasons**

Some Political parties hire hackers to monitor their opposing parties and get their systems data so they can know the plan and plan the successive actions of the opposition. For that, the hackers send fake or blank SMS containing trojans. If any member of the party opens this message or sms from party-owned devices then the remote connection between hackers and victim is established and hackers send different commands to get the data like location history, sms, phone calls, and other PII data.

The victim thought that this was a useless message and didn't contain anything. The message itself has an encoded virus that gets activated after opening such a blank sms. If the victim opens this sms from party-owned devices, then the party's data is also at risk because the phone is connected to the other party's members and the party network. So in this case, all information is leaked by this small mistake

3. **Monetary Gain**

Monetary gain is the most probable reason to hack. Black hat hackers mostly hack users' data for financial gain. These hackers first hack users' devices via different hacking techniques and then sell the data on the black market or publish it to the hacking forums. So that they will get the money against data theft. That is why data breach happens and the stolen data is not publicly accessible, it will be accessible by only Tor Browser.

## 4. Competitive Advantage or Enmity

This is also a dangerous reason. Usually, this happens between one company and another competitive company that has better market value and more customers. The other company hires hackers who need to keep an eye on the competition and their competitor company, what they are doing, what's the next plan, and other confidential business information like product manufacturing process, chemical formula, or proprietary software.

In this case, a competitive company sends their agent as a new employee and the employee is now part of the other company. So as an employee of the company, they can access company information and other data. So they can steal and send this data to the opponent company. This technique is called *social engineering!*

Mainly these are the top 4 reasons why hackers cause data leaks or why hackers hack! After a data breach or data leak, the company's market value, share price, and customer trust has decreased and the company even gets legal notice to violate compliance and secure design principles. And they have to pay large fines in lawsuits. So the company will be in financial disaster or bankruptcy. So hope you understand how data breach affects consumers' data and companies.

Not only companies, but the government also faces data breaches. You will find a lot of news containing information about Government departments that have been hacked, and their websites, portals, and servers that have been down during the hack. The data breach only happens due to a specific vulnerability, and the vulnerability can be technical, software-based, configuration fault, human error, or some other physical factors. So by taking these factors seriously, organizations may protect themselves against data breaches and lawsuits.

# Responding a Data Breach

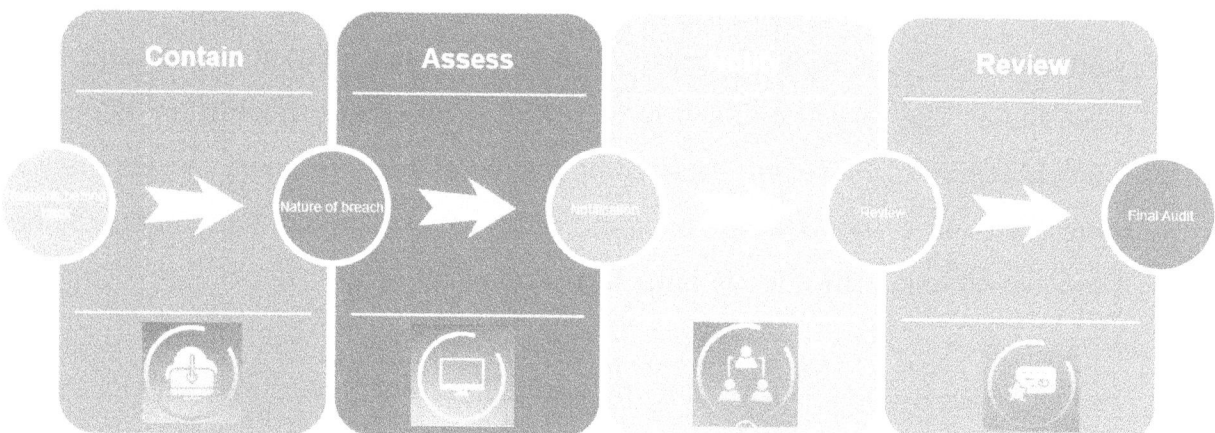

Fig:2.1: 4 Key steps to investigate data breach

We have seen how data breaches happen and what the reasons behind those breaches are. Now we see how to respond properly to data breaches. There are four key steps to handling a data breach incident and responding to it thoroughly.

## 1. Contain

Containment is done when someone suspects that a data breach occurred but is not confirmed! Evidence that suggests a data breach is collected at this phase. Evidence can be web server access logs, emails, network traffic, software configuration modification, any activity that indicates compromise, IP Address, etc.

Based on the evidence, the exact date and time of the incident are predicted and noted for later use and report. Then quickly identifies the reason that leads to a data breach like software vulnerability, configuration problem, phishing emails, multiple failed login attempts, etc.

## 2. Assess

In this phase, which assets are affected by this breach and who is the target! For which users are affected by the data breach is addressed. Moreover, it is recommended to collect how many types of personal information have been leaked, if leaked data is in plain-text format or encrypted if encrypted, and if there is any strong encryption used or encrypted with normal salt. Then note down the suspects who are involved in this data breach! like who is directly and indirectly involved in this data breach?

Then isolate the breached environment from the unaffected environment and move to the next phase.

## 3. Notify

Then notify users that are affected by the data breach and report it to government authority with collected data. Changing passwords is also a good option if passwords are compromised or reused. This process must be completed within **72 hours** because if you make this happen late then the fines may be increased or applied in case not applicable earlier. After this process, create a new incident response plan based on current pain points and past mistakes. If you already have an incident response plan then analyze when this has failed and why this has not worked?

## 4. Review

Make a yearly audit plan and hire an external cybersecurity firm to perform vulnerability assessment and penetration testing and red teaming assessment of the whole IT infrastructure, so vulnerabilities can be mitigated earlier and the risk is predicted earlier before they turn into breach cause! Implement a new Incident response plan if you have not implemented it in the earlier phase.

## How to Protect against Data breaches?

Here are the recommendations and protection measures to prevent data breaches.

- Update all software components with the latest versions
- Train your employees for cybersecurity awareness
- Implement Incident Response Plan
- Take ISO 27001 Compliance for your organization if applicable. This will reduce the chances of such types of mistakes and misconfigurations. And moreover, if an organization is ISO Compliant and still faces a data breach, then this organization doesn't need to pay any lawsuit amount to the government. That's the main benefit.
- Perform VAPT and Penetration Testing both by an internal security team and hire a dedicated cybersecurity firm to do this. That periodically checks and fixes vulnerabilities in technological systems. If possible, also conduct a Red Teaming Assessment because it will predict how your incident response plan works against breaches and how well you're prepared for cyber disasters. You can hire dedicated red teamers to do this.
- Take multiple backups, one is on on-premise servers and the second is a cloud server, which is isolated from in-premise IT infrastructure.
- Implement SIEM Software which takes notes of security events and alerts the security team.
- Perform cybersecurity awareness training, especially for your end consumers. You can conduct webinars, and events to do this.
- Don't fully trust your employees or consultants, they make mistakes too. So make a watch on them.
- Make strict policies not to bring untrusted devices and not to store confidential information anywhere. Use a password manager to do this.
- Hire a dedicated Compliance Officer and Chief Information Security Officer that will be responsible for the organization's security.

# Chapter 3: The DETECT REMOVE ENFORCE Approach

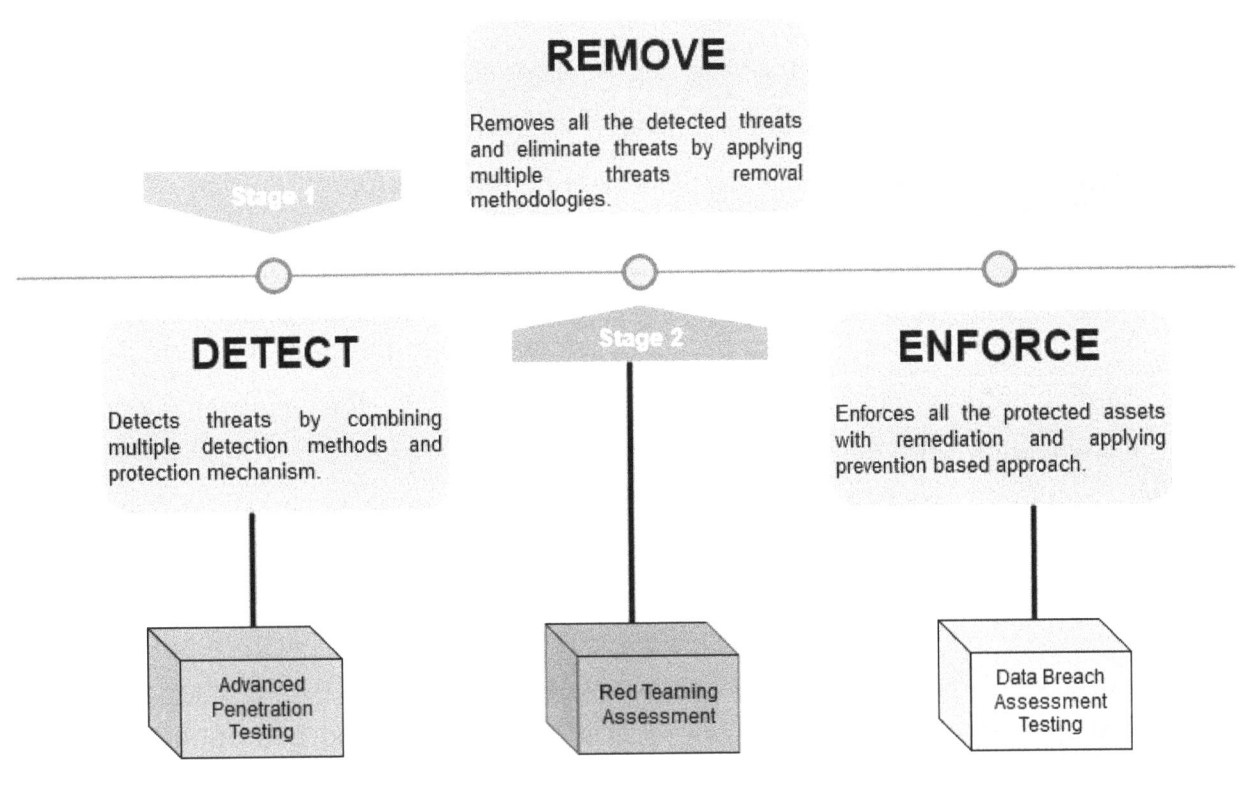

Fig: DRE Approach & Meaning

## What is DETECT REMOVE ENFORCE and How is it helpful?

**DETECT REMOVE ENFORCE** is an approach for cybersecurity. Usually, this approach is applied when other traditional approaches and methodologies don't work. Let's understand by taking an example,

ABCD Pvt. Ltd is a fabrication and steel company that manufactures steel and fabrication products like Iron Rods and metal elements. They have a team size of about 200 people in their 2 factories located in Ahmedabad, India. They hired a cybersecurity firm to assess their digital systems and infrastructure.

The cybersecurity firm secured the organization but they didn't ensure proper safety measures and warranty. After 6 months, an unknown group of hackers hacked this company's website and online store. The company has an online store in which customers can buy products online and also the company has an online payment gateway integrated with its internal payment mechanism.

The hackers use carding techniques to misuse the website's shopping functionality. They somehow found stolen data of customers from the dark web and they launched a carding attack against the company website. So the company notices unusual transactions and random orders from random locations. So they worried about this concern.

*After a few days,*

The Payment gateway company files a legal dispute and chargebacks to ABCD Pvt. Ltd. So both parties are in trouble.

Then ABCD Pvt. Ltd hires two firms, one is a cyber law firm which is dealing with international cybersecurity laws and regulations. And the second one is a cybersecurity consulting firm, which ensures proper safety and periodic audits of the company's infrastructure.

This cybersecurity consulting firm performed a thorough audit and applied some patches to the software. The firm is using a newer technique named ***DETECT REMOVE ENFORCE approach.***

In this approach, they first find known and unknown troubles that are harmful to the organization, remove those troubles and vulnerabilities and then apply prevention-based mechanisms to implement cyber attack resistance.

After this security patch implementation, the cybersecurity firm performed two tests, first is a Red Teaming Assessment, which is ideal to assess an organization's capability against attacks and survival techniques. And the second one is Data Breach Assessment Testing which is special to check and assess parameters that are liable for data breach and data protection. After this process, the firm also implemented cybersecurity laws and regulations compliance like ISO 9001:2015 and NSIC License, so the access controls are properly maintained!

So hope you understand how to DETECT REMOVE ENFORCE Approach works and how it is implemented! DETECT REMOVE ENFORCE technique is the combination of RTA (Red Teaming Assessment)+ APT (Advanced Penetration Testing) + DBAT (Data Breach Assessment Testing) Advanced Penetration Testing ensures a full audit and no vulnerability exists. Which is a DETECTION-based Approach. Red Teaming Assessment ensures an organization is ready to face attacks and it denotes the capacity for how the particular organization survives cyber attacks. Which is a REMOVAL-based approach.

Data Breach Assessment Testing ensures there are no loopholes and no weak areas in particular organizations. So Which is ENFORCEMENT based Approach.

## How does the DETECT REMOVE ENFORCE Approach help to implement Anti-Hacking Security?

Well, this approach works in almost any type of situation whether it is pre-hacking or post-hacking. In Pre-hacking there is a need to secure an environment with almost all perspectives in which Vulnerability Assessment is helpful to diagnose all these vulnerabilities. Moreover, after VAPT, it is recommended to perform Penetration testing which determines how much damage caused by an attacker if they exploit a vulnerability and what is the real impact of vulnerabilities for a specific business, in other words how exploitation of a particular vulnerability damages a business?

In Post Hacking scenarios, Apart from Penetration Testing and VAPT, Red Teaming and Data breach assessment also helps to identify future attack scope and how an organization prepares for a sudden cyber disaster!

And the Traditional approach just only covers VAPT or Penetration TEsting but the **DRE (DETECT-REMOVE-ENFORCE)** Approach contains all of these, so maximum scope covering is possible and provides much solid resistance against cyber attacks.

## Is this helpful in preventing Data Breaches?

Of course, it helps to implement anti-hacking security. If you have implemented DRE Approach then it is said that you have completed all the measures to secure your organization, and in the Enforcement phase, there is Data Breach Testing, which helps to identify parameters that leads to data breach and if exists helps you to remove all of these with ease. Whereas the traditional approach only ensures vulnerability assessment and patching. So this is how DRE Approach helps CISO to build secure infrastructure and prevent a data breach.

## Why to use this DRE Approach?

The traditional approach only contains Vulnerability Assessment & Penetration Testing whereas the DRE Approach contains **Application Penetration Testing + Red Teaming Assessment + Data Breach Security Assessment**, which ensures more safety and maximum security. Detecting threats first, removing detected threats, and enforcing further protection. Which means all-star protection.

## Why does the Normal Protection mechanism work in the short term but fail in the long term?

The normal or traditional mechanism works in short term but failed in the long term, let's understand by taking an example,

There are two companies named **Alpha Pvt. Ltd** and **Beta Pvt. Ltd**. Both are working in the same industry and have the same workforce size. Company Alpha and Beta both have outsourced cybersecurity consulting firms that take care of their organization's security.

Company Alpha tends to use a traditional mechanism and normal approach to protect its infrastructure whereas company Beta tends to use DRE Approach.
They're operating as usual for a couple of years,

After some years, there was one incident that happened for both companies. Both companies are targets of WannaCry Ransomware and all the company's data are encrypted and hackers asking for ransom amounts to be settled in exchange for decrypted data.

Company Alpha tries all the known and traditional ways to get the data back but fails badly. They have backup files but the file is not protected and not encrypted, so their backup files were also encrypted.

Company Beta already implemented DRE Approach into their organization, so they are aware of these types of incidents and disasters. So they immediately shut down all the operations for 2 months and started to remove infections. Fortunately, they have the latest backup stored in the End-to-End encrypted cloud, and the cloud storage is already encrypted with a Multi-factor authentication mechanism. So ransomware doesn't affect the backup files. They have two advantages here. First, they have encrypted backups placed in a cloud environment and second, the cloud infrastructure is isolated and miles away from the company location.

So in these two scenarios, you have seen how both parties responded to sudden cyber incidents.

Due to Normal Protection, company Alpha is badly in trouble. So in this case, the normal approach works in the short term, but not for more complicated and long-term problems.

Company beta is using DRE Approach, so they're protected both in short term and long term. DRE Approach works because it ensures every single point of security and proper planning, so there is less than **a 5%** chance of failure! So hope you understand why normal protection fails in the long term!!

# Chapter 4: Cybersecurity Threats

**What are cybersecurity threats?**

Cybersecurity threats are malicious programs or codes that are intended to be harmful to a particular system. The motive of it is to steal something, gain unauthorized access, and data theft. Threats can be in any form such as malware, spyware, Trojan Horses, etc.

Each threat is designed by black-hat hackers to fulfill some purpose.

For example,

*Trojan Horses* are designed to gain unauthorized remote access to target devices.

*Spyware* is designed to monitor and spy on user activity on victims' devices.

*Malware* is designed to destroy users' data in multiple ways, so users can't access their data whenever needed.

**How do Cybersecurity threats cause data breaches?**

Well, cybersecurity threats cause data breaches in multiple ways. Let's understand one by one by taking examples.

## 1. By gaining unauthorized access:

This is the most common way to commit a data breach. Basically, there are two types of unauthorized access, the first is digital or computerized and the second one is physical. Whenever someone or an unauthorized person tries to trespass or unlock security controls of physical security by interfering with the biometric lock or harming security guards, then it is said to be physically unauthorized access. Whenever someone or an intruder tries to bypass computer or digital security controls by exploiting a vulnerability or exploiting weak configuration then it is said to be digital unauthorized access.

*For example,*

Alpha Hospitals are the biggest private hospital group in the city. They have advanced technology and a proper staff of qualified doctors, specialists, surgeons, nurses, and ward boys. They also have an online doctor consultation booking website and mobile app for their patients., on the COVID-19 Times, they're very busy serving their patients, so all staff is working towards helping patients and their family members. So by taking note of this matter, a group of thieves has planned for a robbery at hospitals. So they came with Guns and Bombs and tried to frighten people at their gunpoint and they asked medical staff to hand over all the available cash. So this is an example of physical unauthorized access.

In Summer times, the hospital organizes discounted medical camps for their patients and non-patients. So they open a booking website and app. So anyone can use the online booking feature by using their website. After some days, a group of hackers hacks their website and plant malware, so the patients cannot access the website and mobile app to book their consultation with the specific doctor. So this is an example of digital unauthorized access.

## 2. Organizations' threats

This threat is also referred to as an internal threat. Let's understand by taking an example,

Gamma Pvt. Ltd is a software development company serving its global clients. They have a total of three offices, the first is in Bengaluru, Karnataka Area, second is in Singapore and the third office is in Dallas Area, United States. The Headquarters office is India's office. In India's office, there are a total of 400 Employees working in different departments. In the software testing department, there is one employee who is not friendly to the company because he carries their HDD and Pen Drives to steal data from the company and sell to their opponent company. One day the company notices their activity and fires this rough employee. In this scenario, the employee causes a data breach, because the employee is an important asset of any organization and they also know the company's secrets and business information. So they can sell to the competitor's company for monetary gain and profits. So this causes data leaks and ultimately causes data breaches.

This is the second most common reason for a data breach. Let's understand by taking an example,

Test Pvt. Ltd is a Graphic design company serving consumers across the globe. They have one office in Ahmedabad Area and 50 Employees working in the organization. Their staff doesn't have any technical members. So they don't implement access controls and online security. On the day of the company's anniversary, a newer employee deleted some files mistakenly and unfortunately, they don't have any backup of it. So the website is broken and inaccessible.

In the above scenario, Data Loss is caused by Accidental Deletion. In some cases, companies use different online services to rely on their operations. So they're using AWS, Azure, or Google Cloud for most purposes. In rare cases, the company forgets the security of AWS buckets and makes them open and accessible to all who have valid links.

So if an attacker gains this link somehow and modifies this link by deleting the data then the Cloud infrastructure may be unavailable to the company itself.

In this case, Data loss and data breaches are caused by accidental and sudden data leaks and loss by external factors.

### 4. Sudden natural disasters

Sudden natural disasters also cause data loss. Floods, Earthquakes, etc cause heavy physical loss. Any organization has its company infrastructure and physical assets like servers, firewalls, Switches, and other precious components. If Earthquakes or floods happen then they mostly damage their physical infrastructure and if a company doesn't have any backup plan or backup assets then it is troublesome for both customers and the company.

### 5. Sudden cyber disasters

Cyber disasters mean digital security threats. Let's understand by example,

QWERTY Pvt. Ltd is a Pharma company that manufactures cancer and autoimmune disease drugs. They're operating the company as usual but someday an unknown hacker hacks the company's website and tries to break their automatic operations. So in this case, cyber disaster is the hacker.

Cyber disasters can also be in other forms like DDoS, MITM, etc. Which are as dangerous as other cyber disasters.

## 6. Exploiting of Vulnerability

Exploiting specific vulnerabilities causes data breaches. Like MITM is Man in a middle attack that causes network traffic sniffing and can capture credentials over the network. DDoS is a Vulnerability that affects normal data operations like websites or mobile apps by overloading servers with random packets. Account Takeover is a vulnerability that indicates that a user account is taken by someone else, this happens when a hacker somehow steals the user's credentials and session ids, and after this hacker changes passwords and removes old session ids. So users cannot access their accounts.

Ransomware or malware is a threat that damages data that belongs to the end user. Phishing is an attack that fools users with an identity, like a fake bank's website. The user doesn't know the website is fake because look wise it is the same as the genuine one. And if a user-supplied credential is over there, then this malicious website sends these credentials to the hacker and the hacker can now log in to the victim's account.

SQL Injection is an attack when a website or mobile app's database is vulnerable to code injection. This means a hacker can inject SQL commands and then grab critical information from the database. In some cases, hackers are even capable of harvesting the whole database, which is a big problem for any organization.

## How do threats bypass normal data breach protection?

Organizations either don't care about cybersecurity or pay less attention to cybersecurity. So they implement very poor cybersecurity controls. For example, Some companies only carry Vulnerability Assessment even after they know VAPT only covers basic assessment and security checkups. Nowadays, Threats are smarter with Artificial Intelligence and becoming more sophisticated each day. Whereas most organizations rely on just single software named **"AntiVirus",** they forgot that Antivirus protection is signature-based, so if a virus changes its pattern using AI then signature-based algorithms couldn't detect these types of polymorphic threats.

So they can easily bypass computer security controls. Antivirus doesn't have a self-defense mechanism, so the virus first tries to defeat the antivirus either by changing its behavior or terminating the antivirus process.

That ultimately leads to data loss and data theft. AI can change the poster of cybersecurity that's true but the AI can also harm cybersecurity that's also true. Because cybersecurity threats are becoming smart day by day, just single protection or normal protection doesn't provide resistance against data breaches. So it is recommended to apply the DRE Approach as we discussed in the previous chapter.

## Types of cybersecurity threats:

### 1. Malware

It is specific malicious software or program and it is designed and developed by black hat hackers to fulfill their purpose and automate some of the tasks commonly used by hackers.

It can cause disruption to a particular service, software, or server. Typically the closest friend of a black hat hacker.

Often used by black hat hackers to disrupt the running systems. Malware contains specific instructions set to perform non-standard computer tasks such as deleting or damaging system files, infecting registry keys, preventing software from running and causing a blue screen of death which is the most common pain point of victims.

Fig: 4.1 Malware

*How malware causes data breach?*

Malware causes data breaches by exploiting some standard system processes and binding itself within processes and starts infecting files and folders. Some malware is often capable of infecting the boot sector, which makes computers unusable and unbootable. After infecting files and folders, it starts slowing down the system and causes frequent operating system crashes, finally sending data back to the hacker and the hacker can steal the user's data using malware. Hackers usually plant malware and by using it, they perform and control remote devices.

## 2. Ransomware

Ransomware is software or program designed to make user files and folders unusable. Ransomware uses strong encryption algorithms and communication protocols which cannot be defeated by standard antivirus engines. It can only be detected and removed by AI/ML Powered Antivirus which is capable of decrypting files using malware's structure. Ransomware encrypts user files and folders and encrypts with common extensions like .booa, ecc, exx, etc. After encrypting the user's files, it starts populating a banner like in the picture below, your files are encrypted, and you can get the decryption key and your files back by paying just **XXX amount** of Ransom money.

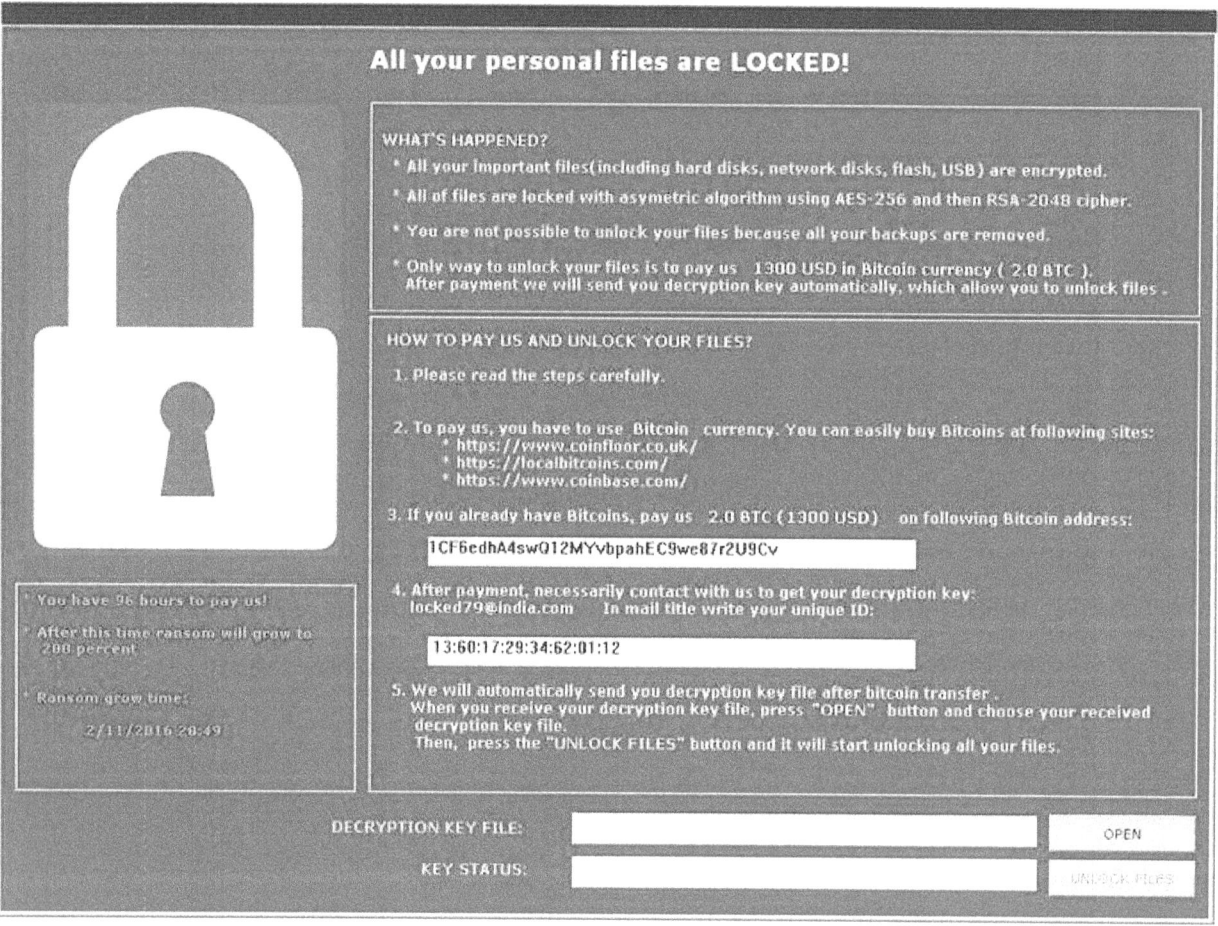

Fig: 4.2 Ransomware Attack

Cybercriminals usually take this payment via Bitcoin and some other cryptocurrency, so the transaction cannot be traced or reversed. If a user fails to pay the ransom amount, the decryption keys will be automatically deleted from the hackers' servers and you permanently lose your files. If the user pays the ransom amount, then they delivered the keys via secure email which is also not traceable. Then the user needs to supply decryption keys to that ransomware program and then the program starts decrypting files again.

Nowadays, ransomware can be removed with newer antivirus which can analyze files without running them in any type of environment. It uses **AI/ML** to detect and predict threats. Antivirus decrypts user files if decryption keys are stored in RAM memory which can be only utilized by ransom programs.

How Ransomware causes Data breach?

Ransomware first encrypts user and system files with powerful encryption keys. Then it asks the user to pay a ransom amount, if the user fails to pay the amount then they encrypt the file forever and your data has been published online for sale on the dark web. So this is how ransomware causes data breaches.

**3. Spyware**

Spyware is basically designed to spy on user activity. Which is often used by cybercriminals to track and monitor users' activity. When a user downloads free programs and software or user downloads cracked or patched software from an unknown website, the software package may contain one or more types of viruses, which get activated after running the software file. Usually, these types of files have a common extension named "**.exe**" which means executable file.

Cybercriminals target people in random order. So they select victims based on social profiles. They have a properly trained team to do this type of extortion crime. Generally, users have a tendency to accept friend requests and follow requests from an unknown girl or lady profiles. If the victim accepts follow requests and friend requests then they send nude pics or vulgar items of the random girls and ask to initiate sex chat with them. If the user starts chatting then they carefully ask the victim for their private pics and videos, if the victim also sends private images and videos then they now have the things they want!

Now they start blackmailing the victim and ask them to pay a heavy amount of money, if the victim refuses to pay that amount of money then they leak private things like videos and photos of the victim to their friend and publish it online. If the victim is not strong enough to survive in this type of circumstance then they may commit suicide!

**4. Trojan Horses**

A Trojan horse is specifically designed to have multiple features like spreading malware or controlling remote devices or sending some commands to the attacker. It is just like a multifunctional malware program. Generally when a user downloads software programs from unknown websites or clicks unknown email links then the user opens session data, saved credentials, and other information being sent by a trojan program.

Trojan horses can control remote computers with just a single click. Whenever a user installs free software and runs into their system then this unknown software silently installs the RAT (Remote Access Trojans) Program and runs in the background. So the user thinks that this is the downloaded software. Now hackers can control user computers and steal data and then later use it for blackmailing and money laundering purposes.

There are different types of Trojan Horse Virus like,

- [ ] Banking Trojans
- [ ] DDoS Trojans
- [ ] Remote Access Trojans
- [ ] Exploits Trojans
- [ ] Backdoor Trojans
- [ ] Fake Antivirus Trojans
- [ ] Trojan-Ransom
- [ ] Trojan-IM
- [ ] SMS & Spy Trojans

How does Trojan Horses cause data breach?

Remote Access Trojans first install spyware, malware, and keylogger programs in the background, so they can be used for different purposes like credentials stealing and carding, etc. Then backdooring the user's system, so it can allow other threats to be entered and spread virus infection.

After this process, the hacker steals and leaks the data of the victim and that is how the data breach happened!

## 5. Hoaxes

Hoaxes are viruses that have suspicious behavior and are designed to confuse victims with different pop-ups and advertisements. So users can make wrong decisions and click and run that unknown resource. Any kind of fake announcement, Porn Images, and other weird stuff. Usually, it uses black, Yellow, and Red Colors so users may get panicked and those who have epilepsy, this color combination is harmful and leads to brain stroke and ultimately leads to death.

### How Hoaxes Cause Data breaches?

Hoaxes are delivered via email attachments, fake websites, fake announcements, and porn websites. If a user visits any of the following fake websites, then they can get hoaxes as a surprise gift. Then Hoaxes start displaying weird images and videos to the user making them panic and those who have weak hearts, also get heart attacks!

After displaying weird content, it confuses the user and if the user clicks that fake resource, then all the data may be either destroyed or delivered to hackers. So this is how hoaxes cause data breaches.

**6. Adware**

Adware is usually delivered via advertisements like clicking on unknown ads or fake product announcements. Adware alone is usually not harmful as malware or trojan but it may install other stuff that puts your computer at risk and data may be in danger.

The main disadvantage of adware is it makes your devices slower and buggy even if you have high configuration and high-end devices. It crashes your web browser and even your operating systems.

### How Adware causes data breaches?

Adware is delivered via automatically generated advertisements and sponsored content, when a user shows interest in that content and clicks on the fake content then adware gets installed and it installs further weird stuff and makes your pc laggy and slow. Then they can install malware and later transfer your files to the hacker. So this is how adware causes data breaches.

## 7. Worms

Worms are a more serious threat after trojan horses. It can corrupt the user files, install backdoor software to allow hackers to gain unauthorized software, consumes high hardware resources, and finally crashes our devices. It usually spreads via Emails only. Once hackers send offer or jackpot emails to random victims, then if any of the victims click on that attachment and run into their computer then worms get installed into their systems and spread via other emails. So if a user sends a new email to another user the worm gets automatically attached and the second user also gets into this trap.

How Worms Cause Data breaches?

Worms spread via email and can read user emails and transfer them to hackers. This is how worms cause data breaches and data theft.

## 8. Rootkits

Rootkits are specially designed for gaining remote access in different ways. If it fails, rootkits try another way to get into this! Once they gain unauthorized access to the victim's computer, they're looking for financial information like credit cards, banking information, and other credentials. This is a stealer of credentials and passwords. Rootkits are also called Password stealers. If users have financial information saved into that device whether into browsing history, saved items, or storage then rootkits have the ability to identify this type of content and make copies of it, and then send it to the hacker.

*There are multiple types of rootkits, including,*

- ☐ Hardware Rootkit
- ☐ Firmware Rootkit
- ☐ Kernel Rootkit

- [ ] Memory Rootkit
- [ ] Application specific Rootkit

How Rootkits caused data breaches?

Rootkits are installed by opening attachments, clicking phishing links, or visiting porn websites. After this rootkits install the Remote connectivity feature and start to establish the connection between hacker and victim, then it is looking for financial information and if found makes a copy and sent to an over-secure channel to prevent antivirus eavesdropping.

## 9. Keyloggers

Keyloggers are software programs designed to capture live credentials and live sessions. Rootkits capture pre-stored content, whereas keyloggers capture live keystrokes and keyboard movement.

There are multiple types of Keyloggers including,

- [ ] API based keyloggers
- [ ] Form grabbing keyloggers
- [ ] Kernel and OS based keyloggers
- [ ] Hardware keyloggers
- [ ] Acoustic keyloggers

How Keyloggers caused data breaches?

Keylogger first observes user activity, whenever the user activity starts, they get activated and start observing keystrokes from contact forms, websites, programs, and other mediums. Then it is stored in proper files and then sent to the hacker. Now hackers can see which website is opened by which time and other activities also. This is how keyloggers cause data breaches.

## 10. Botnets & Crypto Miners

Botnets are devices that include laptops, PC, IoT devices, mobile devices, and other hardware devices that have been recently infected by bots and became part of the botnet network. Botnets are the main reason for DoS or DDoS Attacks. Which is very dangerous at times if not stopped. Because one infects another and so on.

How Botnets caused data breaches?

Botnets were first targeted by hackers, the hacker decided to network, range, and functions. Then it starts replicating as fast as it can by infecting several devices. After this, these infected devices are also part of botnet networks. Now they have the power to destroy any type of strong network and any type of server infrastructure. After they completed their work, hackers targeted specific organizations and launched distributed denial of service attacks which cost millions of dollars to companies and governments. After DDoS attacks they cause data breaches and leak data of the company This is how botnets cause a data breach. Botnets are also used for the cryptocurrency mining process.

# Chapter 5: Implementing Cybersecurity for Individuals

Here there are a total of 15 strategies and ways. If you follow all ways step by step you're much stronger and less susceptible to any type of cyber disaster.

## 1. Keep your all devices up to date

It is recommended to keep your devices up to date whether you're using them personally or commercially in your organization. The devices include Laptops, Android Smartphones, Tablets, iPads, iPhones, Desktops, IoT devices, Smart Home Devices, etc. The hacker mainly looks for loopholes and loopholes that exist because of out-of-date software, Firmware, and Buggy code.

In Standard Cybersecurity frameworks, it is classified as *"Using Components with Known Vulnerabilities"*, which means you're using software that contains out-of-date and vulnerable code and software components.

*For example,*

Mr. Harry is using a total of 3 types of devices for personal use, one is an iPhone, the second is a Windows Laptop and the Third is an Android Tablet. All devices are built on different platforms and run different Operating systems.

They have no problem at all since they bought those devices. But back in Y-2020, in COVID Times, Device manufacturers identified very serious spyware programs and vulnerabilities in All three Platforms **Android, iOS, and Windows**. So Mr. Harry receives an email in the early morning saying you need to update your all devices urgently.

But they denied this email and deleted it. Mr. Harry thinks, Who will hack their data, and even if they hack, what did they gain?

One day, he found that all his devices are operating slowly and they ask their friend who is a cybersecurity expert. So this expert checked their devices and found that all their devices are monitored by a spyware program and hacked! So he panicked! And asked his friend what to do! His friend says,

You must keep your devices up to date because hackers gain access to devices using known security bugs. So Mr. Harry realizes their fault and asks to clean their phone. So this expert recovered the devices and handed them over to Mr. Harry. So Mr. Harry says Thank You, My Friend! From now on, I will take this matter seriously!

Now Mr. Harry is serious about their safety and privacy so they regularly update apps and system software and use only genuine software. He also read articles on cybersecurity updates and News!

As Mr. Harry is now a hero and fully controls their privacy, you can also become a hero and take this seriously.

## 2. Use security software if you're end-user

It is recommended to use Antivirus software if you're an end-user. End User means you're not a technical expert! You think, "So what about technical people, can't they use antivirus software?" We say, Yes, They can! But they're smart enough to handle situations and handle threats! For non-technical users, it is advised to use software like a password manager, antivirus, and phishing website blocker. Because they're not aware of these threats.

Antivirus software has many features like parietal control if you have a child, who uses devices for their education, so you can restrict some apps for the child. It has built-in

Access control features, so you can ban some phishing websites, restrict other users to see what you're doing with the internet, and encrypt the network traffic. It also has malware and virus scanners that can detect multiple types of viruses and insider threats.

Here we compiled a list of the best antivirus if you're an end-user! However, both types of users can use this.

*We compiled this list according to the user reviews and protection efficiency.*

- Kaspersky Antivirus **[Recommended!]**
- Quick Heal Antivirus **[Recommended]**
- BitDefender Antivirus
- Norton LifeLock 360
- ESET Nod32 Antivirus
- Malwarebytes Anti-Malware **[Recommended]**
- Microsoft Windows Defender

### 3. Use All in one password manager for storing passwords

Password managers are an ideal choice for both types of users whether tech-savvy or end-user. Whether it is personal use or commercial use. You're using lots of online accounts like Facebook, Twitter, and LinkedIn with other work accounts. So you can't use the same passwords for all of the different accounts because, if someone hacks your password, then they can gain access to other accounts as well. Also, you cannot store passwords in the disk itself, because anyone can open, read or copy this! Especially when you have a corporate job and all accounts belong to the company. In this situation,

Storing passwords and using the same password for all accounts is not an ideal choice. So in this case you can use a strong password manager. Password managers also warn you about breached websites and warn about password complexity. Password managers encrypt your passwords and notes by using stronger encryption algorithms and passwords can be seen using a common password, biometric unlock, or OTP.

We have compiled a list of the best password managers both personally and commercially.

Password managers not only generate strong and complex passwords but store them in encrypted form, provide the auto-fill capability, check for breached or stolen passwords, and work on Android, iOS, Windows, Mac, and Linux in every platform.

- 1Password **[Recommended]**
- *VP Password Manager [Our Developed]*
- Keeper password manager
- Zoho Vault **[Recommended]**
- NordPass **[Recommended]**
- Lastpass
- BitWarden
- Dashlane

### 4. Implement or turn on Multi factor authentication

Mostly you have seen that all online providers of accounts will ask you to turn on 2FA or MFA, you think, What is this? Well, this is Second-factor authentication which will be required to enter correctly after entering your passwords. Just strong passwords are not recommended. To add an extra layer of advanced protection, it is recommended to enable multi-factor authentication.

Multi-factor authentication secures your online accounts against prying eyes and hackers and also adds a security layer. So if you're using a password manager to use online accounts and your passwords are somehow stolen or leaked, in that case, your account is locked till you enter the OTP code or provide the correct two-factor authentication code.

Multi factor or Two-factor authentication can be in any form, like

1. **SMS OTP Based**

    This is the most common MFA/2FA and is available across all the account providers. This is a very basic 2FA. In this authentication method, the user needs to enter a six to 12-digit unique numeric code which is sent during the login process by the application itself to your registered mobile number.

    In some cases, the application provider asks you to enter an alphanumeric code which is a combination of numbers and alphabets. Usually, this type of OTP is valid for several minutes like 15 minutes, 30 minutes, 1 Hour, etc. After this old code expires and does not work anymore, you need to provide a new code to proceed further.

    For example, **038653, 65430-25435760,xhhg773h9**, etc.

2. **TOTP based**

    TOTP is the second most popular, secure, and cost-effective Second-factor authentication. In this method, the user needs to enter a time based 6 digits numeric OTP on the login page to proceed to the next. Usually, the OTP expires in 60 seconds. Here are some apps that support Time-based OTPs and are available free of cost to end-users.

    To set up this type of authentication, you need to scan a unique QR/Barcode generated as per each user account containing a 12-15 digit unique alpha-numeric key. This key is the identifier of the user account and which account. TOTP looks like **the "012345"** format.

We have compiled the list of mostly used and popular OTP generator Apps.

- Microsoft Authenticator
- Authy - Twilio Authenticator **[Recommended]**
- Google Authenticator
- Zoho MFA **[Recommended]**

3. **Application Specific Passwords**

App-specific passwords are used when there is a need to establish a connection between two apps to exchange, transfer, or sync data. App-specific passwords are look like the following,

App passwords are valid for 1 year or as per use, decided by the user. One unique app-specific code is avoided for specific apps only, this code does not work for other apps. For other apps, you need to generate another app-specific code.

For example, **ioti-4670-jfeh-389h-3b59v**

4. **FaceID [Unlock using your Face]**

FaceID is mostly used by Apple, but also used by other providers. In this, the user needs to scan the face and verify each and every angle of the ace, then capture movement and then submit. After this whenever the user tries to log in, the user needs to enter passwords first and then the app scans your face to verify authenticity.

In some cases, the app doesn't recognize a bearded face. So make sure to be careful to use this. In the recovery method, you have to set up a password, in case your face is not visible or not recognized now you can unlock your device or log in with the password.

5. **Fingerprint [Unlock using your fingerprint]**

Fingerprint lock is basically used in high-security areas when normal passwords cannot be used or face recognition methods cannot be used. Some account providers and smartphones provide biometric unlock methods for their customers. In this method, you need to enroll your fingerprint, and in the backup option, you need to enter a password. So a password can be used when an app or device doesn't recognize your thumbprint.

6. **IRIS Authentication [Unlock using your Pupils]**

IRIS is the most secure method to authenticate users. Which is only used by government agencies and high-security areas like server rooms and also in banks. In these high-security areas, there is a need to add an IRIS unlock method after the biometric lock. So maximum security can be ensured. You remembered that Aadhar cards have both your fingerprint and IRIS authentication stored along with SMS-based OTP.

7. **Hardware Tokens with X.509 Keys**

Hardware token is used when there is a need to identify peoples or authority correctly with their signature. The person's data on signature is stored in digital certificate format and later can be used to authenticate and verify people. In this method, the user needs to generate a digital certificate in X.509 Format and bind it to a USB drive then it can be used to verify people.

You probably noticed that This digital Certificate-based authentication is used by all Government Departments and workers along with CAs and Attorneys. There are multiple types of DSCs available for a single purpose like Income Tax Filing Only and multi-purpose. Like GST Filing, Trademark, Patent Filing, ITR Filing, Tender filing, etc. The validity varies from 1 year to up to 3 years for a single DSC.

8. **One Time Login Links**

Companies nowadays use a One Time magic link that is sent to the user's email and the user needs to click on that link to log in to the application. The link contains a unique session id which can be linked with the user's identity. This is also called a password-less login method and is mostly secured only if the application's code is properly secured. If the code is buggy then a hacker can modify application logic and login into the victim's account by modifying the parameter value.

We have compiled a list of the best hardware based MFA methods.

- Microsoft Azure Active Directory
- Okta Adaptive Multi-Factor Authentication **[Recommended]**
- Imprivata OneSign
- SecureAuth Arculix
- Yubikey Auth **[Recommended]**
- RSA SecureID Access **[Recommended]**

*5. Train yourself against cybercrime and cybersecurity awareness*

This is the most important point of all of the above. Because you need to train yourself, no software or no program makes you hack-free, you have to be smart enough to handle this type of situation. As you have seen in the above example, Mr. Harry doesn't take security seriously and all his devices are spied on and hacked, after this incident he decides to update and train himself for cybersecurity threats.

You can take a cybersecurity awareness course by yourself by searching on the internet. If you're a corporate employee, your employer will arrange this type of awareness session at each quarter end, so you can attend these sessions and educate and train yourself.

The government also launched a cybersecurity awareness camp and free training for the general public, so the general public can take advantage of it and remain secure in this digital world.

You must know in situations when you receive spam emails, receive calls from a bank asking you to provide your OTP and credit card number, followed by an unknown lady on Instagram when she might be spying on you or may make false allegations against you. In the above situation, you need to be careful and immediately reach out to the nearest cyber crime cell with valid evidence that you have been hacked or extorted by blackmailers. People usually don't take action when someone creates financial fraud or blackmails them for fear of society, but it is better to be strong and aware in this situation and take proper action.

You can take cybersecurity awareness courses on the internet.

We have compiled a list of the best cybersecurity awareness courses from different publishers.

You can enroll and get trained free of cost and also you will get the certification of completion.

- Cofence online cybersecurity awareness course
- KnowBe4 Kevin Mitnick's cybersecurity awareness training
- WebRoot Security Awareness Training
- ESET Cybersecurity Awareness Training
- Ninjio cybersecurity awareness training & course
- Cofense Phishing Awareness training
- SANS Institute's cybersecurity awareness course
- Proofpoint's cybersecurity awareness training

## 6. Read latest cybersecurity news and keep yourself up to date

This is also an important point in cybersecurity awareness. As you train yourself to stay safe in the world of the digital era, you also keep yourself up to date with the latest online cybersecurity news. There are multiple websites and apps in which you can learn the basics of security and read the latest articles. Articles include what is happening in the cybersecurity industry, like how cybercriminals find new ways to hack into particular systems, and how the federal government intelligence agency and FBI arrested and seized websites of ransomware gangs?

And most importantly, you can also read about security flaws found in different devices and different platforms. And remedial measures to overcome problems caused by security vulnerabilities.

By reading online security news and training, there is less chance of being hacked and trapped again, because you will put all your efforts into not being involved in any unfair manner in any way. However, no remedy and solution are 100% effective but this will provide preventive measures to stay away from these.

We have compiled the list of best online cybersecurity news websites, in which not only you will get free cybersecurity courses, but also read articles on various topics that are trending and critical nowadays!

- https://www.itsecurityguru.org/
- https://www.scmagazine.com/security-weekly-blog
- https://thehackernews.com/
- https://www.infosecurity-magazine.com/
- https://www.troyhunt.com/
- https://taosecurity.blogspot.com/
- https://www.pcworld.com/
- https://www.wired.com/

The highlighted websites are recommended when you will get all the updates in one place.

*7. Never use public networks for any reason*

This is the utmost reason behind massive cyber crimes. All cybercrime starts with the Free Wi-Fi Network. Often you're traveling to other cities or using airports. And Airports and Cafes offer free Wi-Fi for their customers. But here the game starts! There are so many people using Wi-Fi at the same time and it is a chance for hackers to also use this!

*Let's understand via example,*

The most interesting part is: Airports and Cafes have very tight security because no one knows when an unknown incident happens. So they are very careful about this matter. So they often set up a proxy, VPN server, and Firewall, So all traffic goes through this proxy or VPN server. So they also keep an eye on their customers. They're doing this surveillance for security reasons and they also respect customers' privacy.

When a hacker is also in a cafe or airport and using the same Wi-Fi network, he may set up a network sniffer or something else. They also hack Wi-Fi networks to watch what's going on!

So suppose someone is operating their net banking account from a cafe, the hacker intercepts this request or sniffs the traffic and then monitors user activity, as soon as a user enters a banking website user id and password, the hacker captures this and logs in before the end user login! Now hackers can withdraw all the money by doing online transactions.

In other scenarios, hackers can hack the proxy server and directly view plaintext requests and browsing history. So in this way, hackers also get all the user's details.

So it is advised to use a VPN service while using public Wi-Fi at Cafes, Restaurants, and Airports. And if possible, try to avoid them. Instead of this, you can use your mobile data to complete your work. This will be beneficial for you as no one can intercept your mobile data's network traffic. Because it is routed through multiple servers and is constantly changing your IP address, hackers cannot hack into this.

So hope you understand how the use of public Wi-Fi can put you at risk in multiple ways.

## 8. Never trust anyone

You must not trust anyone for security reasons. Because this overtrust makes you fool and your data may be at risk. Here we understand by taking an example,

You're using Facebook very frequently and spend 3-4 hours on facebook and in other words, you have a facebook bug! You share almost ¾ pics every day with different poses and content. But you're an end-user and don't know about the security risks of using facebook. You accept every Facebook request you receive. This is not a good habit.

*After some days...*

You receive a friend request from an unknown person. The person tends to be a friend of a friend. He is saying that he got your reference from another mutual friend but when you say which friend, this man refuses to say the clear name of that person.

So you're worried about who this man is! But as you have a habit of accepting each and every request you receive on Facebook, you also accept this request. You're a family man and have a young and beautiful wife and have 2 kids. This person starts sending messages like quotes and some jokes. So you often react to their posts. Now you think that he is your closest friend. And you share your internal matters with this person. And this person gives advice to you in problematic situations.

*After some days...*

This man planned to kidnap your 2 kids. He regularly sees your posts. That your kids are going to school at 12 pm in the afternoon, so this man kidnaps your kids from the school grounds and no one sees it. After this incident, you're in trouble and filing a police complaint that your kids are kidnapped by an unknown person. You never see this person in real life, because you never met them anywhere. Also, there is no profile photo of that person.

After some days, you received a phone call from a private number asking you to provide 25 Lakhs Cash in exchange for 2 kids. Otherwise, this person kills your small kids.

So you planned to give them money but the police are following you in a hidden way. When you give money, the police catch that person and try to identify them, after lots of investigation, the police found that this person is your Facebook friend.

So you regret your Facebook addiction and decide to remove this friend and after this incident, you never respond to unknown requests. So hope you learn a lesson from this incident.

## 9. Implement Backup & Restore Plan

This is a prevention-based approach. If you have a backup and restore plan, you can have good recovery power. Let's understand by taking an example,

You're the owner of a fabrication and steel company. In your factory 50 Workers are working. Your annual turnover is 1 - 1.5 crores. You're happy that you're doing good in your business. But from a security perspective, you're the end user. So you have zero knowledge about cybersecurity.

There are server and computer systems in your factory. In this department, there are 5 additional workers. You never take any backup of your important data because you aren't aware of these cybersecurity threats.

In the server room and computer system, there is all your data stored like customer records, accounting and billing data, past orders and future signed orders, payment data, and trade secret business documents.

*After some days…*

There are ransomware attacks in your systems. So all files are destroyed and your reputation in the market also decreased. So you're worried about this matter and decided to hire a cybersecurity firm. The Cybersecurity firm first asks the factory owner if they have any backup of data, and the owner says I have never taken the backup of my data.

Somehow the team recovered data and took a backup to the cloud. And after this incident, the Factory owner realized his mistake and decided to buy a backup and restore software for their factory. So he bought software to automate this backup and restore process. Now the factory owners are tension free.

So from this incident, hope you learn the importance of backup and restoration. We have compiled a list of the best backup software for business and individual use.

- Macrium Reflect **[Recommended]**
- Acronis cyber protect
- EaseUS Todo Backup **[Recommended]**
- BackupAssist
- Windows Backup
- IDrive Online Backup
- MSP360 Managed backup **[Recommended]**
- Veenam backup software **[Recommended]**
- CrashPlan
- Qlik Replicate backup **[Recommended]**

## 10. Don't visit unknown websites and don't download unknown apps or programs

You often have a tendency to try new software and visit random websites. You don't have any antivirus software installed. One day you're searching for a website that offers pirated software and movies. You're amazed because you think that by using this website, you will get all stuff free even for paid content like movies.

So you started to download cracked software from this website. And browse for more software and you also downloaded 3-5 more software which is very costly. So you're happy that you can use this software free of cost.

But as you install the software in your software, your system gets a virus infection. And this is not a deletable or recoverable virus, because it is a polymorphic virus. And you then install antivirus software to scan your system, but the antivirus system says your system is clean and free from viruses.

So you're worried and thinking, what should I do next? So you formatted the PC and then go to a retail store and buy a Windows license and antivirus. And install it on your system. You asked the shop owner if I have had this type of incident in the past. So the shop owner says never install cracked or patched software, because it may contain viruses. So you realize your mistake and decide to install and buy genuine software only. And you then stopped visiting this website. After some days, you heard that the website owner was arrested for a film piracy racket and you think, thank god, I'm free from this stuff!

So hope you understand how this can ruin your life! So stay safe and use only genuine software. And don't support film piracy, watch it on the big screen in the theater.

## 11. Use VPN while using critical services

It is recommended to use a VPN service while using critical services like banking, and paying bills online. Nowadays, people are using UPI Apps like Paytm, Google Pay, and PhonePe to fulfill their daily needs. These apps offer great security and a fabulous user experience. But some are using websites to pay bills. Like Property Tax Bills, Paying Income Tax, etc.

So when you pay bills like municipality tax, property tax, natural cooking gas bill, paying income tax or even recharging your mobile, use a VPN app then pay the bill. This will add an extra layer of security and there is no chance of hacking and intercepting even if you're paying bills from public Wi-Fi like Airports and Cafes.

VPN will route your traffic to multiple servers and encrypt your connection, so no one can know which websites you're using or how much online shopping you did in the last month. Nowadays VPN providers provide great features like No logging policy, End-To-End encryption mechanism, etc. So it is very useful while using online banking websites.

We have compiled a list of best VPN Providers.

- Daily VPN **[Recommended]**
- Nord VPN
- X-VPN **[Recommended]**
- VPN- Super Unlimited Proxy **[Recommended]**
- Turbo VPN
- Proton VPN **[Recommended]**
- ExpressVPN
- TorGuard VPN

## 12. Avoid opening unknown emails and attachments

Email Attachments and Links may contain viruses or something dangerous. Nowadays phishing is very common and people are becoming victims of phishing because cyber criminals use different tactics to trap the general public. As you have seen in the 10th point, how much danger is to open unknown links or download unknown programs from unknown websites. In some cases, cybercriminals send emails like Change your password, because it is compromised even if it is not! But due to fear, you open this link and this link is asking you to allow access to the Microphone and camera. So you panicked so you also allowed these permissions. After this, there are chances they're watching you. You're being watched by anyone. And if you're changing clothes or taking a shower, don't carry your phone while doing these activities. This also applies to children.

If this trap happens to any lady or woman there it is more dangerous because someone is watching and recording that you're changing clothes. If someone gets this clip then they also upload it to youtube or somewhere else and your reputation is totally ruined in this case. So we advise you to not use your devices in your personal living room. Instead, use them in stores or drawing rooms, which will be effective. And if possible,

Cover your laptop, and phone camera with a black cloth. So even if someone is turning on the camera then they only see the black screen and your privacy will be protected.

So hope you understand how this can be dangerous. Clicking on an unknown link or attachment will cost you more than your income in multiple ways. You have seen this in the above example.

## 13. Never give your personal details to anyone

Giving personal details will also cost you a lot. Here we can understand by carefully reading this,

Mrs. Harpreet is a housewife who takes care of their family and her day starts and ends with the family as a typical housewife does. She also uses Facebook to make friends and she also uses Instagram. She is a photoholic and would like to click photos in different outfits. Someone commented on that photo saying **"Gorgeous Punjabi beauty!"** So as a typical woman's nature, she is also hungry for care and love from the public side. So she responded with a comment saying: **"Thanks, Dear!"**

That person sent a direct message to that woman on Instagram asking to give her number. She denied that request but they again asked and now she replied with a number.

Now this person sends inappropriate messages and videos to this married woman and also harasses her by calling her repeatedly. So this woman was in tension and asked her husband what to do next, her husband launched a police complaint and the police arrested this guy. So We hope you understand how sharing personal information with unknown people will cost you more, especially for women and ladies.

## 14. Never visit to DarkWeb

Visiting the dark web will also cost more. Whether you're a man or woman or kids. The Dark Web is just like an underwater mystery. The internet you see and surf is hardly 5%, the rest is the dark web. All illegal work is being done using the dark web and Tor browser. Normal privacy-concerned persons and journalists use the Tor browser, and cyber criminals also use the Tor browser to visit hidden websites.

With the Tor browser, you can visit different websites that are not accessible by any browser like **.onion** websites. These are dark web links. All illegal work like Child Trafficking, Weapon dealing, Smuggling, Terrorists, and Film piracy is done using Dark Web Only.

So it is not recommended to use the Dark Web. Because the CBI, FBI, and other federal intelligence agencies keep an eye on these websites and networks. So you'll get into trouble even if you're innocent.

You can definitely use the Tor browser but don't use it to visit the dark web, which will land you in big trouble. So hope you will understand how this can be troublesome and dark! For privacy, use Firefox with VPN service and proxy, which is enough to hide your identity on the internet. And you can also use Virtual environments like VMWare to hide totally. Suppose, you're visiting a shopping website and you need to hide your identity for privacy reasons, so you may use Linux inside VMWare, if someone tracks you then they only see that you're using Linux. But in reality, you're on a Windows machine. This is how it works!

## 15. Report to nearest cyber crime cell if you victim of any type of cyber crime

This is the last but not least point. If you followed all the above points and still you're a victim of any type of cybercrime, then it is recommended to report it to the nearest cyber crime cell. Nowadays sextortion, blackmailing, and Honey traps are very common, so the general public needs to be careful while using the internet. If you follow the above points and implement them, then there is less chance to get trapped.

As discussed above, in the 12th point, if your private video or photos leaked online then don't get panicked, and don't commit suicide. Suicide is not an option. We know this is not easy for any woman or even for men. Collect all possible evidence, be brave, and fight against cybercrime by reporting it to the cybercrime cell. You can ask the police to hide your identity, and the police will help you in this matter. So we hope you will understand how to report crimes to the cyber cell.

# Chapter 6: Implement cybersecurity for business

*Why is there a need to implement cybersecurity in business?*

Well, cybersecurity is essential and recommended for both personal and commercial purposes. As you understand the importance and value of cybersecurity on a personal level, let's understand how cybersecurity helps businesses to stay secure.

Personally, only your data and your privacy will be covered but in business, there is also the involvement of financial risk, market reputation, data and privacy of business partners, data and privacy of clients, data, and privacy of investors, your employees privacy and data and last but not least is company's data and compliance!

So personally, if you're a victim of cybercrime then it is said that there is only your data and privacy at risk. Whereas in business lots of parties and people are involved, so there is more need for cybersecurity in business than personal.

As you have seen a lot more examples in previous chapters that show individuals and business victims of cybercrime and how they got hacked! Even after putting in sufficient effort, they're not able to secure and defend themselves against hacking. Moreover, cybersecurity helps small, medium, and large enterprises to reduce operational costs and current situational awareness.

Suppose your organization doesn't implement cybersecurity and you face a data breach or any other disaster then your monetary value, data, shares, reputation, huge loss in business, loss of the trust of investors, loss of customers, compliance violation like GDPR, CCPA, HIPAA, NIST, etc, Your competitor company takes an advantage of the situation and try to defame you and your organization, high operational and manpower costs, physical/electronics damage and much more. So it will cost you more and with this cost, you could have implemented cybersecurity for hundreds of businesses. Also, there is a chance of being fined by government and federal intelligence agencies.

If you lose all of these, then it is almost next to impossible to come back into the market and start serving your consumers again. So hope you understand how a lack of cybersecurity in business will put you and your company at big risk.

*How to implement cybersecurity for business with these points?*

Following these key points will help you to deploy cybersecurity step by step. And don't skip any of the points as this will increase the chance of being hacked again! This process is lengthy and time-consuming and takes a couple of days to complete but you will get all the benefits after deploying this. So let's start to understand one by one.

*Phase 1:*
1. **Deploy and implement traditional cybersecurity**
2. **Quick Review**

*Phase 2:*
1. **Deploy and implement cybersecurity by using DRE Approach**
2. **Quick Review**

*Final Review and Combining both methods*

*Phase 1:*

This phase will include all the traditional points that help to stay secure at the ground level but don't ensure advanced security. But it is necessary to deploy the basics before implementation of the *Advanced DRE Approach-based cybersecurity*.

## 1. Deploy the traditional cybersecurity

### 1. Installing and running business antivirus and endpoint security

This is the most basic and essential practice that ensures ground-level security. You must have antivirus software for business. Use only software that is specially designed and engineered for business needs and has the capability of scanning using AI/ML Algorithms. In previous chapters, we have included that antivirus is not mandatory, but this statement is only true on a personal level. At a commercial level, there is a need for top and world-class antivirus software because you cannot keep watch over all the devices and all organizations. So there is a need!

Running regular and scheduled scans is an added advantage because it will detect more and more risks and threats.

### 2. Don't allow employees devices to being used in company infrastructure

Don't allow employees' devices or BYOD(Bring your own device) policy. Because this will put your company at risk. Because no one knows which employee is doing wrong with the company's confidential data and assets. Instead of this BYOD, implement and make available only organization devices with properly defined access controls.

### 3. Train your employees against cyber crime and arrange cybersecurity awareness workshops and seminars

It is also necessary to educate and train a company's employees whether you're running an accounting firm or running a law firm. This will reduce crimes like phishing, smishing, Vishing, identity fraud, and data theft. For this, you can conduct different seminars and workshops. And also you can participate in external conferences and workshops organized by other companies as well. So this will tell your employee how to respond in case of cyber urgency.

4. **SafeGuarding your physical infrastructure by installing CCTV, Biometric devices and security guards.**

Installing CCTV cameras and safety hidden cameras is a must. Install CCTV in every room, floor, and corridor. Install hidden CCTVs in sensitive areas like a server room, and boss cabin to keep watch on employee activity. For this, you can use Timesheet and Employee Software. So this will integrate with CCTV and provide you a more detailed overview of your company.

5. **Strong Backup and Restore Policy**

A strong backup and restore policy is also a must. This is a very basic requirement. You can use Automatic business data backup software that automatically takes weekly, monthly, quarterly, and yearly backups and stores them in a cloud environment which is an isolated environment and also makes sure the software has encryption capability so it can encrypt the backup with the strongest algorithms. One backup is stored on a premise backup server and one backup is stored in a cloud environment. At least this can be implemented if you don't have the budget to buy CCTVs and Antivirus. Nowadays some cloud providers provide end-to-end encryption with Multi-factor authentication, and you can subscribe to their plans and buy additional cloud storage.

6. **Updation of software used by organizations along with upgrading of hardware whenever necessary.**

Upgrade hardware whenever necessary, for example, if your servers and networking equipment are out of date then you can purchase new networking equipment like Hardware firewalls, Switches, Routers, and servers. Moreover, keep all your software and data up to date and in a safe place without fail.

7. Carrying out security assessments like Vulnerability Assessment

Use an automatic vulnerability scanner scanned by your internal security team and apply remediation and quick fixes. If code changes are not available then you can apply a virtual patching mechanism in which you can ensure the weakness is covered by security policy or some kind of software.

8. Defining and implementing proper access controls

Defining and implementing access control will help you in identifying the cause immediately. If you have multiple departments like sales, marketing, accounting, and technical then device and make segments in which one department device cannot be accessed by other department devices. But assign admin devices in each department in which other department devices can be accessed.

9. Secure your organization's cloud infrastructure

Secure your backup's cloud infrastructure with multi-factor authentication like encryption keys, hardware tokens, biometric devices, face recognition, etc. By default, most cloud storage provides you to use MFA instantly and securely. But if you use a provider that is not supplying MFA then you can use additional tools to add security level. Not only backups are stored in the cloud but some projects and confidential data are also stored, so it is necessary to deploy an additional layer of security.

10. Strong password policy

A robust password policy is also a must. Set the expiration time of passwords to at least 90 days. So every 90 days the user needs to update and set new passwords for all organization-owned devices. You can use a password manager for business that supports multiple platforms like Android, iOS, and Windows. One can recover a password if lost by someone.

## Quick Review:

If you implemented all the 10 points then it is time to review all of these. For this, you can use reviewing and auditing software to fulfill this purpose. Note down which is not working or which is failing. So you can re-implement or re-deploy all of these. The human mind is full of mistakes, so before launching it, make sure you have tested that it works correctly, if not then modify it wherever necessary.

So hope you understand how traditional cybersecurity helps implement basic protection, but it is not efficient or enough so let's move on to an advanced DRE Approach based cybersecurity.

## Phase 2:

This phase will include how to Apply an advanced or *DRE-based Approach* to secure it properly. So let's start by understanding one by one.

### Deploy and implement cybersecurity by using DRE Approach

For advanced threat elimination, mitigation, and Resistance against more sophisticated cyber disasters it is recommended to implement **DRE(DETECT-REMOVE-ENFORCE)** based approach. Earlier in **Chapter 3**, we understood deeply what DRE is and how it can help. Now it is the time to elaborate in a live environment.

## 1. Advanced Penetration Testing

Advanced Penetration is the process of finding, exploiting, and fixing vulnerabilities. It is usually done in 5 to 6 stages which are seen in the below diagram. It is more than traditional penetration tests and vulnerability assessment because it covers more scope including automatic and manual approaches and is done by multiple experts like VAPT Auditors, Penetration Testers, Red Teamers, and Cyber Forensic Experts. VAPT only covers vulnerability findings but traditional penetration test covers how this Vulnerability can be used to harm the system and advanced penetration test contains how this vulnerability's long-term effect and how it can create more vulnerabilities(Pivoting) and maintaining access. So Let's understand how Advanced Penetration Testing is done.

Fig: 6.1 Phases/Stages of Advanced Penetration Testing Cycle

1. Reconnaissance

Recon basically contains information-gathering stages. VAPT Experts and Penetration Testers gather technical information about the target How many software libraries are used by business applications, and in which platform is built? Which ports are open and how the information is used to identify vulnerabilities, etc.

Recon can be done both manually and automatically. In Automatic Way, different Automatic Tools and Techniques are used to gather the target's information. This is less efficient as the testers need to confirm the vulnerability by manually checking affected areas. In the Manual Approach, testers need to manually run custom build or developed scripts, tools, and techniques to gain information about the target.

After the testers gain useful information, the first phase is over. So the following information is required to move to the next phase.

★ Server operating system used
★ Software components used
★ Open and Closed Ports
★ Filtered Ports
★ Firewall Protection
★ Any other security mechanism like Rate Limiting and IP Blocking
★ Website Technology stack
★ Sessions Mechanism
★ Sensitive Directory
★ Any Blocking Mechanism like Access Controls and IP Access Blocking Mechanism
★ APIs used
★ Subdomain Enumeration

So the above 12 points are needed for complete information gathering. After these testers save all the RAW data and reports which can be used in the next phase.

2. Passive Scanning

Passive scanning is a method in which tools and testers both check how servers respond to requests and how it is handling requests. Includes Automatic Tools and Manual Tools and Techniques. If some security mechanism is there in the back-end system then it cannot detect passive scanning, because passive scanning only predicts app structure, software components, open/close/filter ports, and other stuff. There are lots of tools in GitHub available for passive scanning. Only passive scanning is inaccurate because there is manual confirmation needed from the side of the tester.

After this phase, testers save all the required results generated by automatic and manual tools that are useful in the next phase.

3. Active Scanning

This is the most important part as this will decide how the application is secured. Active scanning also includes automatic and manual tools and techniques like directory, users, database enumeration, parameter findings, etc. Active scanning can be detected by back-end security mechanisms.

The testers need to be careful while doing active scanning as this can destroy database and application files. If some protection mechanism is there and it is blocking requests and manipulation the testers try different ways to bypass this protection mechanism and get into it.

After this, testers find application parameters that can be very useful to test the vulnerability one by one. Now the testers apply Security standard Frameworks like,

1. OWASP Top 10

OWASP is an open-source security organization that standardizes and prioritizes application security and implements OWASP Top 10. It includes different categories of vulnerabilities.

- ★ A01:2021 - Broken Access Control
- ★ A02:2021 - Cryptographic Failures
- ★ A03:2021 - Injection Flaws
- ★ A04:2021 - Insecure Design
- ★ A05:2021 - Security Misconfiguration
- ★ A06:2021 - Outdated Software Components
- ★ A07:2021 - Identification and Authentication Failures & Flaws
- ★ A08:2021 - Software And Data Integrity Flaws
- ★ A09:2021 - Security Logging and Monitoring Failures
- ★ A10:2021 - Server Side Request Forgery

There are multiple years of OWASP Top 10 List available like 2013, 2017, 2019, 2021, etc. But testers are advised to use only the newest list published and follow the list thoroughly. In some cases, testers need to refer to a multi-years list because of the scope and criticality of the business.

2. SANS Top 25

SANS Top 25 is more advanced than OWASP Top 10 and used for more critical business applications. IT is also standard, some companies follow this standard along with the OWASP Top 10's latest list. So maximum security can be ensured. Here is the list of the Top 25.

- ★ CWE-787: Out of Bound Write
- ★ CWE-79: Cross Site Scripting (XSS)
- ★ CWE-89: SQL Injection (SQLi)
- ★ CWE-20: Improper Input Validation
- ★ CWE-125: Out of Bounds Read
- ★ CWE-78: OS Command Injection
- ★ CWE-416: Use after free
- ★ CWE-22: Path or Directory Traversal
- ★ CWE-352: CSRF (Cross Site Request Forgery)
- ★ CWE-434: Unrestricted File Upload with unknown Types
- ★ CWE-476: NULL Pointer Dereference
- ★ CWE-502: Deserialization of untrusted data
- ★ CWE-190: Integer Wraparound
- ★ CWE-287: Improper Authentication
- ★ CWE-798: Use of hard coded credentials
- ★ CWE-862: Missing Authorization
- ★ CWE- 77: Command Injection
- ★ CWE-306: Missing Authentication for high security areas
- ★ CWE-119: Buffer Overflow
- ★ CWE-276: Incorrect default permissions
- ★ CWE-918: SSRF(Server Side REquest Forgery)
- ★ CWE-362: Race Condition
- ★ CWE-400: Uncontrolled Resource Utilization
- ★ CWE-611: Improper restriction of XEE(XML External Entity)
- ★ CWE-94: Code Injection

So as you see SANS Top 25 is more advanced and contains more categories of vulnerabilities and system risks.

PTES is Penetration Testing Execution Standard which is not a checklist but a standard. All phases like the above 6 phases are part of PTES. So here are the 7 Phases of PTES.

- ★ Pre engagement interactions
- ★ Intelligence Gathering
- ★ Threat Modeling
- ★ Vulnerability Analysis
- ★ Exploitation
- ★ Post Exploitation
- ★ Reporting

4. OSSTMM

OSSTMM stands for Open Source Security Testing Methodologies Manual. And it is done using 2 phases: 1st is OSSTMM Channels and 2nd is Phases of OSSTMM.

**Phases of OSSTMM:**

- ★ Work Change Process
- ★ Test Plan
- ★ Test Process
- ★ Reporting Standards

**OSSTMM Channels:**

- ★ Human Security
- ★ Physical Security
- ★ Wireless Communication
- ★ Telecommunication
- ★ Data Networks

5. NIST

NIST is the National Institute of Standards & Technology. It is usually done in 7 stages.

- ★ Identity Management
- ★ Authentication and Access Control
- ★ Awareness Training
- ★ Data Security
- ★ Infor Protection & Procedures
- ★ Maintenance
- ★ Protective Technology

Testers test using rules methods described in the above standard framework. So there is a proper unique method. Testers can choose standards according to the business app scope and industry. If there is a financial app like a banking website or mobile app, then testers need all of these. Testers now prepare a checklist of how and which vulnerabilities need to be assessed by themselves.

## 4. Analysis & Assessment

The analysis basically contains all the analytical techniques used by testers to identify security flaws. The analysis also includes both manual and automatic tools. And moreover, it also includes open-source, commercial tools, and custom-made tools for better detection and mitigation purposes. In this phase, testers detect the vulnerabilities that exist in the system or software and try to reproduce the security issues for later use.

## 5. Exploiting

Exploiting is basically the process of exploiting or the process of targeting vulnerabilities with code weapons. In this stage, testers usually exploit the identified vulnerabilities and then check whether vulnerabilities are exploitable or not. Based upon that, **CVE(Common Vulnerability Exposure)** is decided. CVE is the core that indicates how much damage is done by exploiting this security flaw and how dangerous it is. And also includes that it affects other system resources as well. Exploitable vulnerabilities are classified as Lower risks security flaws. Exploitable security vulnerabilities are classified as high-risk security flaws. Then the tester moves to the next phase.

## 6. Maintaining Access & Clear Traces

This is the last phase of Advanced Penetration Testing. Now finally the tester tries to maintain access with the exploitable vulnerabilities. So that they can assume these maintained vulnerabilities are of critical severity. Testers then classified maintained vulnerabilities as critical vulnerabilities and non-maintained vulnerabilities as high-risk vulnerabilities.

Now the tester tries to clear the traces and prepares the document which includes scope, severity, list of vulnerabilities, recommendations, Proof of Concepts like Videos, Snaps, etc, reproduction steps, and remediation and fixing guide. Finally, the penetration test is marked as done and after remediation from the developer side, the tester team checks again against those detected vulnerabilities and verifies the patch, and mitigates the security flaws. So hope you understand how this is a lengthy, time-consuming, and costly process.

## 2. Red Teaming Assessment

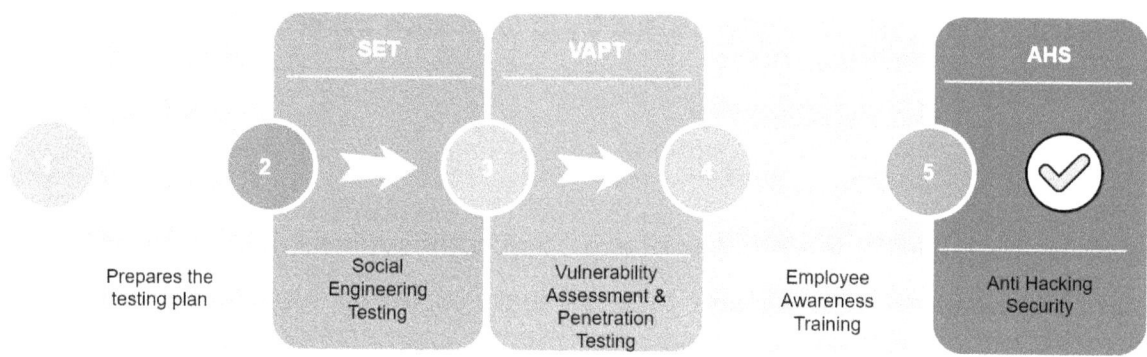

Fig: 6.2 Red Teaming Phases

Red Teaming Assessment is more advanced than penetration test but not only contains technical security flaws but human flaws and other flaws which can also be responsible for a data breach or hacking attempt. Penetration Test only contains technical-related vulnerabilities whereas Red Teaming Also contains more than technical and human-based vulnerabilities. Red Teaming is not ideal for smaller organizations, it is only for medium or larger size organizations that require more than security. As Penetration Test is done in multiple phases, Red Teaming is also done in multiple phases like,

1. Prepares the testing Plan

This is the first phase in which the red teamers and VAPT Team prepare the Plan of what is going to be tested, how it is going to be tested, who is going to test it, and why it is going to test. The testing plan includes the checklist and data needed to start the Red Teaming Assessment. There is no need for penetration testers but a need for VAPT auditors. Checklists and plans include Simulated Attack Testing methods, Social Engineering and Phishing Testing, and a couple of other ones.

2. Social Engineering Testing

Social Engineering is the art of exploiting human minds. Hackers use different tactics to make a trap for their victims and take money from it. As hackers do in a bad way. Red Teamers go unplanned visiting the office which wants to be tested. Now Red Teamers take one place and start working. Only The owner of the company, the security team, and Red Teamers know that they're doing testing. Employees are busy working on their tasks.

Testers send different types of phishing emails to all employees. When employees open their inboxes and try to open the emails and attachments then they have been trapped and failed in their training. Those employees who delete the email or are marked as spam or phishing will be real heroes for that organization. After this phishing assessment testers take notes on how many employees respond properly to that email and How many do not!

During this testing, organizations turned off their anti-virus and other security software as this will create a barrier for this assessment. An assessment is required. The testers will do multiple types of testing including,

★ Man in the middle attack

The man-in-the-middle attack is done first to check how employees react and respond. Testers set up proxy servers which intercept and sniff data and check to steal employees' credentials, how much do employees keep their login sessions open. Then the testers take notes like how much employees keep their accounts open and remain unsecured and how much do not!

Then testers move to the next phase, which is very interesting and also dangerous.

★ Spear Phishing

Then testers targeting those employees are victims of MiTM and Phishing. So they started to target individual employees of an organization and observe how they behave.

★ Vishing

Then testers prepare the list of all the vulnerable employees and then start vishing. Vishing typically involves the process of calling an employee one by one and asking them to provide credentials. Don't be confused here, because hackers or testers don't directly ask for personal information. They use genuine matters like they're calling from XYZ bank and your XYZ account is blocked. So to unblock, provide a full account number with Password and OTP.

So then the testers prepare the list of who are victims of these and move to the next phase.

★ Email Phishing

The hackers try to send phishing emails to employees who are victims of previous tests. Testers send different emails to different employees with the matter of different subjects like JackPot, Banking Document Update, etc.

★ Pharming

Pharming is done after Email Phishing. In this, malicious code is injected into the target's computer, and code is then sent to fake websites by fooling them. This only happens when an employee clicks and opens email attachments to run the program.

★ Spoofing

Spoofing is done by testers to determine how an employee can put an organization at risk. Testers design and deploy fake websites or popular platforms and then encode them to the short form and then send an email asking to open the email to see the friend requests or follow list. So employees feel an interest and try to open attachments within the browser.

VAPT is a vulnerability assessment and penetration testing. You are already familiar if you read the previous chapters. Now testers prepare VAPT Checklists and then start performing VAPT and prepare VAPT reports containing Vulnerability Reproduction steps, Scope, Severity of threats, details of applications, credentials used, APIs, etc.

4. Conduct Employee Awareness Training

After the VAPT, testers conduct simulated malware or ransomware attacks on the system and check how an organization's anti-hacking security works well. If failed then hackers prepare the report based on it and then conduct employee awareness training to train and educate employees based on the tests' final results. For this training, testers can use animated videos and slides to present interactive demos of cybersecurity awareness.

5. Anti Hacking Security

Testers now finally implement different security controls whenever applicable and required and then upgrade previous anti-hacking security controls effectively. And finally, make a present document containing different phases and details with test results. Now finally the Red Teaming Assessment is finished. Testers now implement patches, apply virtual patching, implement firewalls if not implemented before, secure organization, and retest with previous vulnerabilities. If it exists, then patch it again with stronger security remedies. So hope you understand how the Red Teaming Assessment is carried out by VAPT Auditors, Testers, and Red Teamers.

Data Breach Assessment Testing is required when an organization wants to check its defense ability along with responsive handling and a backup plan. It is also performed in multiple phases as Red Teaming and Penetration Testing. There are a total of 5 Phases. An organization went through this to pass this audit. This testing is done only after penetration testing because it is required in the next phase.

*So Let's understand how this is done in 5 different phases.*

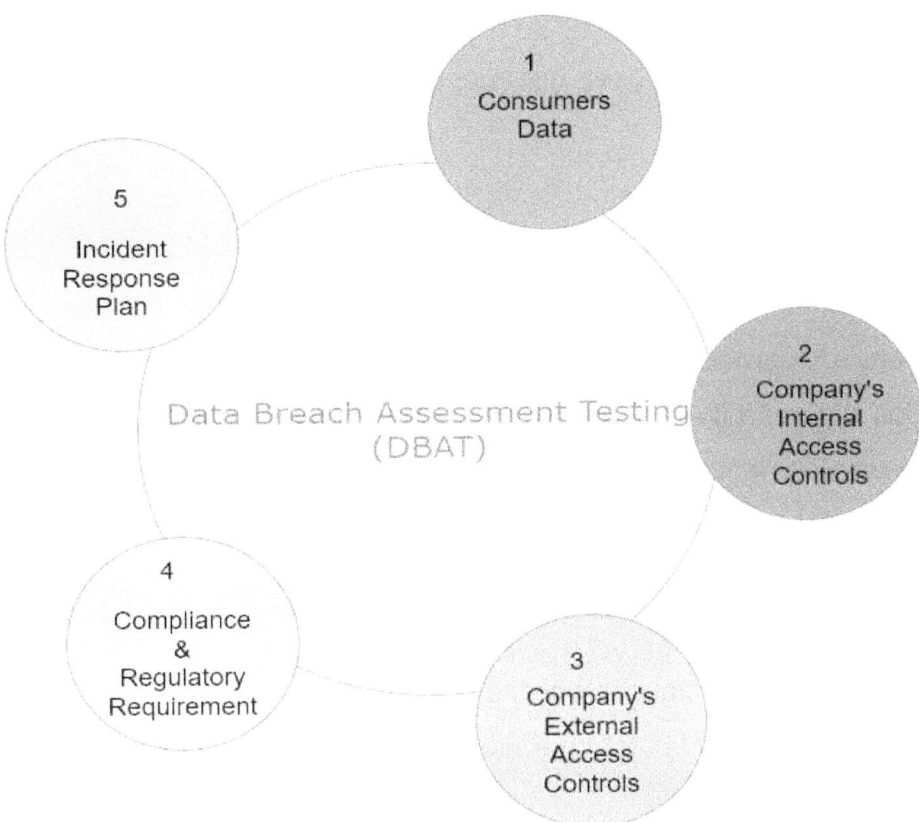

Fig 6.3: Data Breach Assessment Testing Phases

1. Consumers Data

Consumer data can be in various forms like RAW Data, Plain-text, In-The database, encrypted data, converted data, Application format-specific data, etc. In the first phase of Data Breach Assessment Testing, Penetration Testers and Cyber Forensics experts analyze the type of data used by an organization. The types we already see.

*For example,*

Theta Pvt. Ltd is a Legal Firm providing legal services to their clients. So in the legal firm, data can be from different clients that are seeking different services and stored in different formats like app-specific formats. For invoicing and accounting purposes, they're using Tally ERP 9 software. So the data is stored in a proprietary data format which can only be utilized by Tally Software. No other software can render this data. So the Team basically checks different data stored in different formats utilized by different software.

2. Company's Internal Access Controls

In the next phase, the team is going to test access controls used by the company's internal use purpose. Internally how the company operates and handles data and its consumers, which is observed by a team of cyber experts in a live environment. So they can prepare a checklist and start testing. Internal Access Controls include Server Room, Department head's cabins, Network Room, Meeting Room, and other individual department devices.

The team is observing and checks all the above-mentioned points one by one and then prepares notes for later use.

3. Company's External Access Controls

After examining internal access controls, the team moved to the next phase which is external access controls. In this phase, the team examines how companies communicate with their clients, Partners, and Vendors. So all outer access controls including the above ones are observed and monitored by a team of cyber experts in a live environment. After this process, the team prepares notes for later use.

To examine how data breach occurs, the team of cyber experts needs to observe and monitor everything as they cover it. How employees check in and check-out will also be monitored and checked along with the other factors.

## 4. Compliance & Regulatory Requirement

Then the team prepares the compliance and regulatory checklist and arranges meetings with the executives. Now they're discussing how and why there is a need to comply with certain rules and regulations and failing to do so results in what and how.

*For example,*

Theta Pvt. Ltd is a Law Firm so it is required to comply with certain cyber laws. In this case, companies need to have compliance with ISO 9001, MSME, and NSIC Registration respectively. So for this, The team invites external lead auditors that audit companies and issue compliance certification. Apart from these regulations, If the Firm is located inside of the United States, It is required to Comply with CCPA(California Privacy Act). So in this rule, you must not share or transfer information or data of the consumers to another media or format. If needed then it is required to take the consumer's consent and then proceed.
Moreover it is GDPR and is applied globally so the team also implemented it with all the security internal and external controls.

## 5. Incident Response Plan

Now the team assesses the incident response plan if it has already been implemented and if there are any problems then the team starts working on it and fixes it. This is the most important point among all of the above. If a company doesn't have an incident response plan then the team needs to implement this plan. In this case, company Theta Pvt. Ltd doesn't have this type of Plan ready, so the team implemented it from scratch. If the company had previously done Red Teaming Assessment then it is assumed that the company already has an incident response plan. But the company Theta doesn't carry out any Red Teaming.

After the process is done, the team of Lead auditors, Penetration Testers, and Forensics experts review all the implemented points and then finally publish them. And the company is now ready to survive a cyber-attack.

## 4. Disaster Recovery Planning and Data Recovery

If an organization has an Incident Response Plan then it is said that it also has a disaster recovery plan because the incident response plan involves a structured approach to handle unplanned incidents and disaster recovery is also about this topic. The company and the team are now finally working on the Disaster handling process, so all systems, documents, and everything should be under the control of an organization. To check if the plan is working or not, the team of cyber experts launched a simulated attack on Theta Pvt. Ltd. fortunately the organization isn't affected by this attack.

Now finally the team implemented a backup and restore plan and put it on automation. So no one is to blame for the sudden incident and sudden disaster.

There are Total 6Rs' in Disaster recovery planning **Reduce, Response, Recover, Re-Sync, Resume, Return.** So **Reducing** means reducing the damage done due to the unknown incident, **and Response** means how the organization responds to that unknown incident. In other words, it also indicates how well the organization is prepared to face disaster, **Recover** means the recovering capacity after an incident, **Re-Sync** means how much time taken by an organization to get back to normal working operations, **Resume** means resuming capability of an organization after facing sudden and drastic incident, **Return** means how fast an organization recover themselves and get back to the overall recovery.

Data Recovery is a process to recover data from physical or logical damage. And the team also suggested data recovery software so they can purchase and deploy it to the central endpoint server. So by running this software at the endpoint level, all Devices' data can be recovered because all devices are accessible from the endpoint device.

So it is said to have a stronger than normal approach. So hope you understand how the DRE Approach can make a difference and how it is more efficient than the traditional approach.

# Chapter 7: How to save millions of dollars

*Why are companies failing to protect their business even after spending millions of dollars on cybersecurity?*

Well, the company makes the following 5 mistakes: that's why their operational cost for cybersecurity increases?

**1. Companies hire dedicated experts for their own purpose for different roles**

Companies usually hire dedicated experts. Nowadays, many companies that are serious about cybersecurity employ full-time experts for different roles. Like VAPT Auditors, Penetration Testers, Red/Blue Teamers, CISOs, VPs of security, Lead Auditors, Cyber forensics Experts, Security Engineers, Security analysts, security administrators, network security engineers, etc. Companies employ for all of these roles and pay higher salaries. So this will cost more for even smaller or larger organizations. So this will decrease your company's profit margins. And even after they employed so many experts, they cannot stop data breaches or cyber-attacks. Still, the company faces or suffers a data breach.

You read newspapers, so you could have observed front paper news like "X Company suffers from massive data breach and XYX number of user accounts has been hacked or affected by this data breach."

During interviews for these roles, companies look for eligible criteria like experience, certification in their industries, etc. For example, X Company is looking for CISSP-certified Information Security Specialists.

But No certifications will make them suitable for the roles. Their skills, Problem-Solving abilities, and experience make them suitable candidates.

## 2. Company doesn't trust outsourced experts or freelancers!

The second most critical reason is freelancers and outsourced talents can reduce the fixed operating costs of any organization. For some roles, there is no need to employ full-time people. Instead of this, you can hire per hour basis outsourced experts like freelancers.

Freelancers usually have worked with different companies with different projects. So they have more subject-specific expertise and value-adding than normal employees. Freelancers have the ability to do the toughest and hardest tasks with ease because they have good problem-solving skills by default.

Some companies provide freelancers for other companies. So you can hire them on an hourly basis and pay only for what they do and how they do it. No bullshit. Usually, these types of outsourced experts take **50-70$** Per hour charges for cybersecurity-related tasks. Some experts are willing to work on a long-term basis so you can either make them a partner or collaborate with them by signing a contract agreement.

They are even more trusted and challenging than normal employees. Because clients don't pay them if they leave the work in the middle or don't complete the work. So they're always working under pressure and on tight deadlines. Whereas, full-time employees are persons who require a salary on a monthly basis even if they don't work on a single project. So this will add more costs and the company will face more problems. Because more companies' assets are utilized by these employees.

So for occasional needs, An organization employs or hires on-time outsourced experts and freelancers to work with them. This will cut the extra noise and costs. So we hope you understand how this will save you a lot of money.

### 3. Companies use costlier softwares even if it is not needed.

Companies also use costlier software for accounting purposes they bought a software called Tally ERP9, although more cheaper and effective software is available like Zoho Books and Invoice, Ankpal Accounting software, Intuit Books, Vyapaar, etc. So they will cost less than Tally Software and provide you more features with flexible payment options.

### # Accounting softwares Costs:

1. Tally ERP 9 Costs you: **30,000 INR One Time** with boring interface
2. Others costs: **1000 Per month**

Some software is even free for a lifetime and doesn't cost you any money. For Non-GST Complied companies, These software companies provide you software free of cost. So you can use or deploy it on your premises.

As Tally ERP 9, Companies also use Vulnerability Management software like Burp Suite Enterprise, Nexpose, Nessus, Rapid7, etc. Which costs thousands of dollars per year. This software can be replaced by a team of expert penetration testers. Instead of buying these types of software, hire freelancers who work on a contract basis. Let's calculate the overall software costs.

# Vulnerability Management Software Costs:

1. Commercial softwares costs you around: **4000$ Per Year**
2. Team of Experts Freelance Penetration Testers costs you around: **30$ Per hour as per requirement**

As these softwares companies calculate and save lots of money. So We hope you understand.

4. **Companies don't assign a properly calculated budget for security related needs.**

In annual or semi-annual company meetings of board meetings, company executives discuss budget and cost cutting, but they don't discuss cybersecurity budget. So this should be included in the company's board meeting. In this meeting, the executives should decide how much money should be allotted to cybersecurity needs. For Hiring Experts on an hourly basis, some software costs and some operational and hardware costs like hardware firewall, UTMs, and a couple of other resources.

If a company applies these 3 to 4 strategies to save money, they can allot this saved money to the company's growth, like for big assets for the company.

5. **They trust their hired so-called cybersecurity experts!**

When some companies hire quality people they fully trust their so-called expert employees. But in reality, the employee can save money for the company and also an employee can destroy the company. So don't trust your employees and your outsourced staff fully. You're running a company and the company is not only yours. Lots of investors, partners, and other people have invested money to gain profits from it. So by blindly trusting your staff, you will dishonor your investors.

To solve this problem, You can use employee monitoring software and timesheet management software. This will cost you around $50 per month and if you buy a yearly plan you will save hundreds of dollars on it.

So we hope you understand how blind trust can fool you and put your company members at risk. So be practical in business. Don't trust anyone blindly.

We have compiled the list of best employee monitoring software for your business.

- ★ Time Doctor **[Recommended]**
- ★ ActivTrak
- ★ Insightful
- ★ We360.ai **[Recommended]**
- ★ Traqq
- ★ DeskTrack
- ★ Teramind **[Recommended]**
- ★ Hubstaff **[Recommended]**
- ★ VK Control Employee PC Monitoring **[Recommended]**
- ★ FocusRO

How can your organization save millions of dollars?

- Implement all the above 5 points
- Backup everything, all times
- Outsource but smartly
- Keep your employees and staff updated with the latest trends and threats to cybersecurity
- Don't trust anyone
- Save the cost of thousands of dollars by creating a balance between outsourcing and full-time employees. When to outsource and when to hire full-time.

- Organize seminars and workshops at your company for cybersecurity awareness and employee awareness
- Participate in the world's renowned cybersecurity conferences like Black Hat USA, Def-CON, etc and build strong networks.
- Insure your company with cyber insurance
- Win the trust of your clients and Partners along with investors

# Chapter 8: Automation, AI in Cybersecurity

Artificial Intelligence and Machine Learning are trending nowadays and used everywhere like in Software And IT Industry, Medical And Pharma Industry, Finance, Banking, Transportation, Manufacturing industries, etc. And With the use of AI, you can automate Anything like repetitive tasks. With the use of AI/ML integrating with Software, some companies can automate the whole manufacturing process without single hand touch. So this is the most fantastic achievement ever in today's landscape.

In cybersecurity, AI is heavily used because of its smartness. In cybersecurity, AI is used in Threat Learning and Threat Modelling, AntiVirus Signature, Fraud Detection, Smart Authentication algorithms, and Fighting Bots and also AI can predict The chances of a Breach by analyzing the Auditing Report and Organization's structure.

As AI is useful in cybersecurity and helps cybersecurity experts to automate security events and monitoring processes, it also has major downsides like DeepFake.AI, Machine Learning Fraud, Carding, and The Threats are also using AI to be smart enough to defeat antivirus products.

So we people need to understand the Upsides and the downsides of AI and according to it, we need to learn how to use it properly. Because we can't blame any technology for any wrongdoing. All responsibilities are on humans. So Humans need to be more responsible towards technology's merits and demerits.

Nowadays, World's Top AI Scientists and Top Technology People are researching how AI can solve Human Problems which are not easily solvable by humans. As technology grows, crime and fraud also grow.

As discussed in the above paragraph, AI can be especially useful in cybersecurity, and not only cybersecurity it can revolutionize multiple industries. So Let's see how AI can create and change the future of cybersecurity.

I. Cost Reducing with Easy Automation

AI can reduce heavy operational costs like high manpower costs, software costs, cyber insurance costs, data breach costs, etc. AI can take these all very low. In fact, AI can replace Humans in the future, So AI can kill more employees. Because there is only one time cost to implement Machine Learning Model and AI for specific needs. Then All costs will be saved and covered in the next 1 year's timeline. Now more and more companies are adopting AI for their infrastructure and process automation, so they can cut costs, fire employees and keep their customers happy. AI can cut costs because it has the following capabilities:

★ AI can learn from its mistakes
★ It can be integrated with vast mechanisms like Machine Learning, Neural Networks, and a couple of others. Which will extend its usability and functionality.
★ It only has one-time setup and implementation costs. So Pay once and enjoy for a lifetime. It will significantly improve itself by constantly learning from inputs and outputs.
★ It can replace humans and persons with AI/ML powered Chatbots and Customer support agents which can answer almost any question the customer asks within a few seconds of asking.
★ Improve communication efficiently
★ It can standardize and optimize production and factory automation.
★ It can stop cybercrime by predicting data breach possibilities.

## II. Detecting Fraud

AI can be used as a fraud detection algorithm. Nowadays companies hire data scientists, and machine learning engineers to design fraud detection and prevention algorithms that can be used during online transactions. In the market, you will find a lot of solutions based upon AI/ML which can be used as SDK and easily integrate with your software or hardware. Payment Gateway and Financial institutes often use AI/ML to take advantage of it. Let's understand by taking an example.

*Example,*

XYZ Bank is a private bank and they offer various banking and investment services to their customers like debt and equity-based loans and financing, Capital investments, Angel Investments, and Other banking services. So they have almost 10,000 customers and they have 5 branches in the city located in different areas. They have a website which is very old and they don't provide any internet banking facility services.

So they hired software engineers and a cybersecurity experts team to deploy one for them. Now the team is working on the new project and after 6 months the process is finished and cybersecurity experts are now assessing websites for vulnerabilities and fixing them.

After 1 month they also completed their work and were ready for the launch phase. So the bank finally launched this website having internet banking features at the bank's 50th anniversary.

So they arrange one small party and invite investors and customers to take part in this happy moment. After the day of the bank's anniversary, customers provided good feedback and they're gaining new customers as well.

Moreover, the bank is also planning to launch its payment gateway for consumers. So after 3 months, they completed it and tested it and this is working as expected. To integrate AI with the Net banking website and payment gateway website they hired ML engineers and designed algorithms that have capabilities to detect and prevent fraud based on behavior analysis.

So hope you understand how The bank gained an advantage of AI and implemented it for Fraud detection use cases. This is a very important use case of AI. AI can detect fraud and also creates fraud. So better to be careful. Because the capabilities can be misused easily.

III. Threat Modeling And Threat Elimination

This is the second most important point and use case of AI. AI can significantly improve Threat Learning and Threat hunting procedures. Normally These processes are not straightforward. But AI can make it Straightforward and easy by integrating Machine Learning. AI can predict threats in advance, so companies can take action on them.

Nowadays Antivirus companies implement Their own AI Algorithms to detect and remove threats just like an Antivirus company named Quick Heal launched its own AI Algorithm named **"GoDeep.AI"**. They claimed that this algorithm has the capability to detect and remove advanced threats which are not usually detected by normal antivirus programs.

AI can detect any type of cyber threat like malware, ransomware, spyware, and Trojans among others. Because of its learning ability. AI can also learn from the threats detected by it and user behavior so it can add it to the database and make itself smarter and more effective.

## IV. Bot Fighting

There are two types of bots: Good Bots and Bad Bots. Good bots are bots that can increase traffic like Google Bot, Bing Bot, Yahoo Bot, etc. These all are Good Bots. They can increase your website traffic and often increase the sales ratio by increasing the value of a lead to a customer. Bad bots are scrappers who steal the content of any website and make it harder to find for the consumer's side. So this can be dangerous as it can decrease website traffic. And consumers lose interest and trust.

AI also helps in Bot fighting. Nowadays companies try to find a solution that matches their requirements. For the same, Bots can destroy the whole company by gaining an advantage of the scrapping mechanism. Which can only be done using AI. But In this case, AI can be helpful. It can detect IP addresses and other parameters that will help to identify bots. Bots usually change their IP a few times, within 10 minutes. So this is the first note. The bot can also change and manipulate user agents From IP 34.56.3.15 in the first request there is the Firefox browser with Windows OS. And if this request is blocked then the bot again changes its user agents to MacOS and Browser to Google Chrome. And also changes its IP to 56.64.12.98.

During Machine Learning model deployment, ML Engineers make a dataset that contains all the known bots. After this process, they deploy these tools into learning mode for 30 days. In these 30 days, the Algorithm updates itself with lots of other data and automatically updates the dataset. After 30 days, the algorithm is trained enough to challenge the known and unknown bots.

So Now ML Engineers deploy it to a live environment and check that it is working correctly or not. They observed that The algorithm they designed is up to 97% effective in preventing bots. So this is how AI can be useful in detecting and preventing bots.

## V. Data Breach Prediction

AI can be used to predict data breaches as well. You think, how it is possible. So let's understand. A data breach is a serious cybersecurity disaster that can happen at any time and in any place. So there must exist something that will be available **24x7x365** to monitor this critical IT Infrastructure. AI Chatbots and customer services bots along with predictive algorithms can help to predict risks earlier. At first, they analyzed the whole IT infrastructure and generated a score. After this process, AI Algorithms looked for weak areas and updated the score and now finally generates a score that contains predictions and weak parts. It highlights points to be noted and risks that can cause a data breach.

By using this score, Humans can check how much the company is vulnerable to cyber attacks like data breaches. So they can take proper action.

AI can improve incident response handling processes along with Disaster recovery planning. They seamlessly integrate with SIEM and Vulnerability Management software and take data from it and in learning mode. After this process, AI will suggest the weak areas in your incident response plan and why it can fail at times. So humans can correct these mistakes.

In disaster recovery planning, AI can generate scores as it does in a data breach. It can recommend a few points that need to be implemented to ensure maximum security. After this score, humans can implement suggested changes. Note that AI can also make mistakes. So make sure you check the results manually by confirming them. For this, Check the False Positive ratio. If it is high then it is likely that your algorithm is either not learning or has bugs.

So hope you understand how AI can help to mitigate the problems of data breaches.

## VI. Designing Secure Authentication Mechanism

As AI solved other problems that are most dangerous at all times. AI can also solve this problem. AI can help developers to design secure authentication algorithms. Here we understand how.

Software developers use NodeJS, Next.JS, TypeScript, PHP, Python, Ruby, and Perl-like programming languages to establish communication between the front-end and back end. And MySQL, MSSQL, MariaDB, Oracle DB, MongoDB, DB/2 for database handling. The process is very time consuming and requires multiple rounds of testing to provide a workable authentication flow.

AI can help developers to design authentication flow with proper security. There is a requirement to write multi-page code to deploy security mechanisms like encryption and decryption and validation. AI can provide you with datasets that are helpful to identify malicious users who are intended for bad purposes like stealing other users' credentials. AI can throw different challenges at suspects by observing their behavior.

*For example,*

In a previous example of a banking website, They obviously have an authentication mechanism to log in to their dashboards. During the login process, as soon as the user supplied credentials to the login page the back-end logic checks into the database whether the User ID and passwords are correct or not. In some cases, hackers can bypass this logical flow and hack into databases. After multiple failed login attempts with the same IP, AI can ban the rough user permanently or for some time. Due to AI, hackers could not harm the website's back-end part because AI can stop hackers right away.

VII.     Email Spam Filter

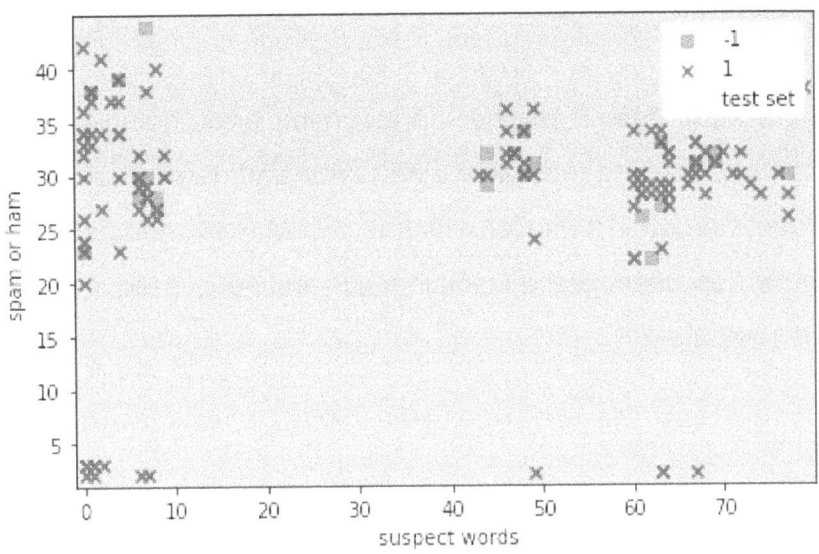

Fig: 8.1 Email SPAM filter

AI can be useful to design email spam filters by providing spam scores. If the spam score is less than X then it classifies an email as a normal email and If the spam score is greater than Y then it classifies an email as spam. But it can be a false positive sometimes due to some problems like email deliverability issues. If the email failed to deliver the first time and the user then tries to send the email again and now the email is sent successfully, now in this case normal Algorithms either skip this email from checking or mark it as spam due to deliverability issues.

To prevent this type of problem, The ML model needs to be trained first and datasets should be updated more frequently. This is the only way.

AI can analyze the content of an email before the user opens the email and marks it as suspicious according to the content type and email sender's reputation score. Phishing can also prevent using AI. AI can use Reputation and behavior-based analysis to identify whether it is from a genuine sender or someone is fooling the user by sending a fake email. For example, If someone is trying to send an email to the end-user with a facebook id Facebook's algorithm will detect and identify the culprit.

Apple also uses AI to detect whether an incoming or outgoing phone is spam or not by constantly analyzing the caller's behavior and details from the internet. As Apple and Facebook do, Truecaller which is SPAM Prevention software available for Android, and ios users are also using ML and AI to predict the SPAM caller and block it immediately.

VIII. Vulnerability Management

AI can be useful in Vulnerability Management. It can automatically classify vulnerabilities and remediation by analyzing the type of vulnerability. Some software vendors like Rapid7 and Nessus are selling their software which has inbuilt AI to prioritize and remediate faster than the normal manual process. It can process thousands of vulnerabilities once and assign them to different testers as fast as it can. AI can detect hidden vulnerabilities, provides better and faster analytics, and eliminates false positives by providing risk scores and confidence metrics.

Most software vendors already provide it as we discussed above. So hope you understand how AI is helping Penetration Testers to find and remediate faster than normal manual processes

IX. Automating Security Compliance & Governance

AI can help to automate security compliance based on your company's industry, employees, and requirements. Nowadays some companies are offering software that automatically audits your organizations and generates Audit reports. AI suggests compliance based on the above factors and provides you with more effective audit reports because it is error-free, contains good suggestions to improve security and meet specific compliance, and much more.

## X. Crime Detection and Prevention

Nowadays criminals find new ways to commit crimes but AI and Technology can stop them. Here is how! Military organizations use AI software that identifies intrusion attempts in borders and keeps watch over the enemies. If someone is trying to trespass the restricted area and enter with dangerous weapons then AI can alert military officers to stop them immediately. After detecting the enemies AI can alert all the departments in the military and the military can take action against the enemies.

Airforce and Navy Departments also use AI to identify underwater activities. Submarines have inbuilt AI software that can identify dangerous threats inside water and alert the navy department. AI can be used here to identify another submarine from the enemy's area. So as it identifies, it sends an alarm to the navy department and they will take action. So this is how Ai can be used in underwater areas.

Federal Government intelligence agencies and other bureaus use AI to identify criminals. The FBI has its own forensic algorithm which helps them to gather evidence based on the type of crime committed by a criminal. Ai can be used to identify objects like guns, Bombs, and other dangerous stuff from different clicked pictures. Sometimes policies click pictures in highly pressured and dangerous environments and pictures may be blurry and not clearly visible. So AI can help them to clear blurred images and identify objects like suspects, dangerous objects, and much more.

Nowadays Cars also have in-built AI software which can alarm the owner if any unknown activity is detected within its radius like a robber trying to steal something or a robber trying to break the car lock. When it is detected it sends a silent alert message to the car owner and the car owner can take help from the police to arrest that robber. This is how AI is used to detect and prevent crimes.

*How AI is contributing to increased cybercrime?*

As you see, AI is helping a lot of different people and different types of industries. But as technology grows, threats also grow and become smarter. AI can be part of serious cybercrime. So Technology should be controlled by humans otherwise bad people will definitely misuse it. As coins have two sides, technology. And AI also has dark sides apart from bright sides. Hackers can use AI to develop sophisticated and undetectable threats which cannot be controlled by any type of security mechanism. So this is a serious issue. Moreover, AI is contributing to increased suicides you think how! S Let's understand by taking an example,

Mr. Yash is a famous businessman and he has built several crores business empire. So their family and their parents are happy. They have an Import-Export business. Mr. Yash is not so tech savvy and they're not technical people as you see in the previous chapter, it is easy to fool end-users who have zero knowledge of technology. One day, Mr. Yash was scrolling Instagram when he received an anonymous follow request and the request was sent by an unknown woman. So Mr. Yash accepts the requests thinking that she might be a friend of a relative or something else. After this acceptance of follow requests, Mr. Yash starts chatting with her daily. Now they're good friends. Although Mr. Yash is Married and blessed with a good wife and two kids.

*After some days...*

This woman is asking to initiate a sex chat with them. Mr. Yash denies this. But this girl again asked them and promised then she won't tell anyone. After some time, The woman sends private images and videos which are very sensitive, and no woman on this planet will share with an unknown person. After this, Mr. Yash panicked and asked her to not send this type of content over social media as he is a reputed person and running a multi-crore business.

The woman then asked to send private pictures of them. So Mr. Yash refused to give it to her. But this woman will now blackmail him and say that if he is not sending private images with her then she will tell everyone that he raped her. So he again panicked. And Mr. Yash is now confused about what to do. After thinking for some time, Mr. Yash denied that and blocked her profile. But this is not enough. The woman is then irritated by this type of behavior and then downloads full images of Mr. Yash from Instagram and starts faking it. She is a professional cybercriminal and she already blackmailed almost 100+ Persons including Mr. Yash.

This unknown woman downloaded some adult videos from a random website and tried to mix them with Mr. Yash's photos. She knows that there is one technique by which she can change the face of the person who is in the adult video. So she did it and made four videos and sent them to Mr. Yash's Whatsapp number.

Mr. Yash again panicked and asked this girl to delete these and not to tell anyone. But this woman then publishes these videos to the internet and youtube and after some weeks, Mr. Yash's business faces huge losses and clients are leaving the company.

So Mr. Yash went into depression as normal people do Mr. Yash cried a lot and then decide to do suicide when he tries to commit suicide, his wife arrives and stop him and then Mr. Yash hugs his wife and cries a lot and tells his wife that he has not done anything wrong. The woman is harassing him. His wife then says Yash doesn't panic and relax, we need to complain to the cybercrime cell regarding this incident, And they are now at the cybercrime cell. Now the officer asks some questions to the couple and finally launches an FIR against her.

After lots of searching, the Police arrest that woman, and then the woman says that These videos are not of Mr. Yash, she uses DeepFake.AI to change the face of the video with the other person. And then finally the police punished this girl with 15 years in prison. And now Mr. Yash's Family is happy and decides not to respond to any unknown requests he received earlier. So we hope you understand how dangerous AI is.

# Chapter 9: Should you trust yourself or your consultants

## Vulnerabilities in Normal Peoples

People have a tendency to skip things that make their mood off or make them bored. So In cybersecurity matter of cybersecurity, the same thing happened. People usually ignore small things that are required to be checked like their personal safety and privacy. People are too lazy to observe what is happening around them. For example, Some people have weak memory and memory power so they save personal things and passwords like PII (Personally Identifiable Information) somewhere as they write in their diaries, or save the details as notes on either their smartphone or their laptop. So this is not a good way to deal with the information.

You learned how a small clue or small information about specific people can be used against them. So even if they know what will happen after they behave like a careless person, they still do the same.

Like if someone has their credit/debit card number stored then they don't need the PIN to do a transaction. Here is how. The thief can use a technique named carding, in the carding attack, there is only a need for a credit card no and expiry date. There is no need to have PIN no, CVV, or Person Name. These can be automatically retrieved in cyber criminals' systems by malware. Carding attacks are harder to detect and stop. There is only one solution, You need to tell your payment service provider to stop payment services temporarily because if you failed to do so, then the reverse chargebacks could happen at any time and in any number. So this is very terrible when you face this type of situation, it is too late to take any action. If you face sudden multiple bulk orders from random people and random locations with random addresses, be careful because this is the trap in which you are caught. So if you observe any type of suspicious activity then it is recommended to inform your CISO (Chief Information Security Officer) and payment services provider. So they can stop services right away.

So here you see how vulnerabilities in people can affect the whole ecosystem and disturb everything in the ecosystem.

## Vulnerabilities in Cybersecurity Consultants

As you see, vulnerabilities in people affect the whole business and ecosystem. Vulnerabilities in consultants also affect business here is how.

Almost any size organization has its outsource and in-house team of cybersecurity experts who take care of the business's cybersecurity needs. These persons include VAPT Auditors, Penetration Testers, Red/Blue/Purple teams, DevSecOps Engineers, Network Security Experts, Data Security Officers, Compliance And Governance Officers, Cyber Lawyers, etc.

These people also have some kind of vulnerabilities by default which makes the whole company vulnerable. When companies hire a team of cybersecurity experts, they either check their background for any type of criminal activity or manually visit the person's house for inquiry. In most cases, the company performs background verification by intelligence agencies to check whether the person is a criminal or not.

But background verifications alone are not enough. Because it doesn't ensure the person is fully trusted. Even after clearing background verification, companies should never blindly trust their consultants specifically for cybersecurity needs. Because in many cases, the cause of data breach is related to the company's employees. So vulnerability in consultants makes not only them weak but also the organization they worked for.

Even after performing VAPT or penetration testing, the consultants think that the organization is now secure and free from cyber attacks. But the hackers still hack their organization and steal the data. So companies should never fully trust their consultants. In this type of case, the company can do the following:

- → Never Trust your employees and consultants in terms of cybersecurity. Because cybersecurity requires Zero Trust!
- → After assessing your organization's IT infrastructure, perform sudden audits by trusted third-party firms so they can test and provide you the results. Because the internal security team has ignored some potential risks but the external cybersecurity firm proves that this can lead to vast data destruction.
- → Take ISO Certification if applicable. Choose standards according to your business activity and industry. Like if you're running a medical diagnosis lab then it is required to have NSIC, NABL and ISO 14971, etc.

## Vulnerabilities in Cybersecurity Companies

Cybersecurity companies also have vulnerabilities. Because they don't ensure maximum security. The DRE Approach and method of utilization of the DRE Approach is a patented and proprietary approach that is only utilized by **The VP Techno Labs® International, which is one of the finest organizations across the world for securing companies against data breach.** Cybersecurity companies apply a traditional approach and as you see in the previous chapters, the Traditional approach is not fully safe. Still, your organization requires assessment by a proper and award-winning cybersecurity firm.

So during hiring a trusted cybersecurity provider, you can consult a business manager to take advice. If you're hiring a cybersecurity firm to do a security audit, you can use _Clutch.co - This is a B2B platform and provides good suggestions. So never ever depends on a single source of protection._ Most firms charge thousands of dollars for a security audit, if you hire a good Indian firm then this will cost less than usual. Within your budget, you will get all of the security features and good support.

# Chapter 10: A Perfect Solution

- Only hire Indian cybersecurity firms even if you're from outside of India. Because it costs you less, is within budget and they have a good history of protection coverage and efficiency.
- Follow all the recommendations given at the chapter ends.
- Never blindly trusts anyone.
- If possible, Use a **DRE Approach** to boost protection efficiency and efficiency.
- Don't depend on Automated vulnerability scanners.
- Understanding the risks of technology and AI and use according to it.
- Always have two incident response plans because one fails, then another saves you from million-dollar fines.
- Implement IDS/IPS, which is a system for intrusion detection and prevention. Which will alert your SIEM and SOC team to take proper action.
- Use Managed Security Services Providers
- Use security patch management tools
- Train your customers and provide awareness training for them.
- Implement Multi Level Identity and Access Management Solutions. You can search on the internet and you will find one for your business.
- Use secure file encryption software to share files and documents between your teams and employees.
- Use Private and end-to-end chat software for internal communication regarding projects.
- Don't store important information anywhere, even not in encrypted form.
- Avoid the **"Secured Enough"** Mentality. No solution is 100% secure.
- Invest more in cybersecurity
- Be honest about what you do with your organization.
- Frequently check whether your implemented anti-hacking security and systems are working properly or not. Keep watch over any suspicious activity.

# References:

**1.)**

Martins, Andrew. 2023. "Cybersecurity: A Small Business Guide." Business News Daily.

https://www.businessnewsdaily.com/8231-small-business-cybersecurity-guide.html.

**2.)**

Joshi, Krati. 2022. "How AI is Changing Cybersecurity: New Threats & Opportunities."

Emeritus. https://emeritus.org/blog/cybersecurity-how-ai-is-changing-cybersecurity/.

**3.)**

"AI in Cybersecurity: Incident Response Automation Opportunities." n.d. SISA.

Accessed April 18, 2023.

https://www.sisainfosec.com/blogs/ai-in-cybersecurity-incident-response-automation-opportunities/.

**4.)**

Martin, Daniel. 2021. "8 Benefits of Using AI for Cybersecurity." Cyber Management Alliance.

https://www.cm-alliance.com/cybersecurity-blog/8-benefits-of-using-ai-for-cybersecurity.

**5.)**

"Tips for Calculating Cybersecurity ROI." 2022. Sanity Solutions.

https://www.sanitysolutions.com/tips-for-calculating-cybersecurity-roi/.

6.)

Devry, Jane. n.d. "5 Ways Small Businesses Can Save Money With Cybersecurity." Cybersecurity Insiders. Accessed April 18, 2023.

https://www.cybersecurity-insiders.com/5-ways-small-businesses-can-save-money-with-cybersecurity/.

7.)

Freedman, Marc. 2021. "Cybersecurity Threat Protection can Save Your Business Money." Expense to Profit.

https://expensetoprofit.com/cybersecurity-protection-save-your-business-money/.

8.)

"15 Essential Cybersecurity Tips for Small Businesses." n.d. Kaspersky. Accessed April 18, 2023.

https://www.kaspersky.com/resource-center/preemptive-safety/small-business-cyber-security.

9.)

"10 Most Important Basics of Personal Cyber Security You Must Know." n.d. Geekflare. Accessed April 18, 2023. https://geekflare.com/basics-of-personal-cybersecurity/

www.ingramcontent.com/pod-product-compliance
Ingram Content Group UK Ltd.
Pitfield, Milton Keynes, MK11 3LW, UK
UKHW050414240426
12048UKWH00020B/1510